Cooking with the Horse and Buggy People Series

Table

for

Rhoda Miller
Sam & Amy Miller

Two

438 AMISH FAVORITES FOR TWO PEOPLE

FIRST PRINTING May 2007 . 5M
SECOND PRINTING August 2007 . 5M
THIRD PRINTING September 2007 . 5M

ISBN 10-DIGIT: 1-933753-02-1
ISBN 13-DIGIT: 978-1-933753-02-7
COVER PHOTO BY: Nic Miller
BOOK DESIGN BY: Regina Beachy
PRINTING BY: Carlisle Printing

2673 Township Road 421
Sugarcreek, OH 44681

Carlisle Press
WALNUT CREEK

The Springhouse

*The springhouse, built by Sam and Amy Miller's
family, into which flows the spring that once belonged
to the first Amish settler in Holmes County.*

THE OLD FARMSTEAD that I grew up on holds a lot of
sentimental value for me. I remember the good times I had with
my siblings, the games we used to play while helping Dad milk
the cows, building tunnels in the haymow and singing songs after
supper. Of such are good memories made! Farm life wasn't always
an easy life—getting up at 4:30 AM in the dead of winter to milk the
cows—but it was a good way to learn family values and to acquire a
good work ethic. Something else I cherish about the homestead is its
place in local history.

In the summer of 1809, only six years after Ohio had obtained
statehood, Jonas Stutzman, a young Amishman, ventured into the
Walnut Creek Valley and set his stakes on what is now my dad's farm.
Jonas must have been an adventuresome fellow, as he was only 21
years old when he built his first cabin there in the wilderness. The
valley had an ample supply of large oak and walnut trees, which

furnished him with an abundance of building materials. Those days were long before the invention of the chain saw—everything was done by the sweat of a man's brow. He was the first white person to settle in eastern Holmes County, Ohio—in the heart of what is today the largest Amish community in the world.

One day Jonas was clearing ground for his cabin when a sprung tree limb he was cutting off kicked back and broke his leg above the knee. What was he to do now? It was five miles over a buffalo trail to his aunt and uncle's place close to what is present-day Sugarcreek. Using the materials at hand, he bound up his leg with thin willow sticks he found growing nearby. Then he fashioned a cane and crutch from some sticks and hobbled his way slowly over the trail, arriving at his uncle Jacob's cabin late that night, where they set his leg. Pioneering wasn't for the fainthearted! It took real grit.

As if being the first settler didn't give Jonas a big enough place in our area's history, he was a rather eccentric person too. He became known as "Der Weiss" or "White Stutzman." This was because in the latter part of his life, out of deep religious conviction, he dressed in all white clothes. Jonas predicted the year 1853 to be when Christ would return to establish His kingdom on earth. He evidently believed his predictions to be correct because he even made an oversized chair for Jesus. This chair can still be seen today at the Amish and Mennonite Heritage Center in Berlin, Ohio.

Although I had no idea while I was growing up, I have learned in recent years that Jonas was my great-great-great-great-great-grandfather. That has made the old homestead even more special to me.

Of course an abundant supply of water was indispensable to frontier survival. This must have surely influenced Jonas to locate his cabin where he did—beside a spring of water flowing out of the hillside. Almost 200 years later, this spring is still going strong.

This spring of water and the fact that it was used by Jonas Stutzman have been the inspiration behind a family project only recently completed. For the past several years, Dad had been talking of building a stone springhouse to utilize the water from the spring. It couldn't be just any old springhouse if we were going to build one. It would need an arched doorway and a slate roof to top it off. After much talk and planning, things finally started to happen in the summer of 2005.

Oh! those stones were heavy, making the work backbreaking, and there were many Saturdays we had to sacrifice for the project. But it was a labor of love and enjoyable indeed to work together as a family to see the realization of a dream. The finishing touches were put on the building in the early summer of 2006.

On the inside of the house the spring enters through a pipe in the back wall, splashing into a basin hewn out of solid stone. The basin is also part of the back wall, being set in a niche. From there the water flows off to either side, disappearing into the wall for a short space until it cascades out of its outlet into pools on both sides of the building then on down to the Walnut Creek.

Traditionally, springhouses were used for food storage before the invention of modern refrigeration, and it was probably as close as the pioneers got to having running water. These days we have no such necessity, but it's still good to see a watermelon or two floating in those pools in the hot days of summer. That is when I like to step inside and find respite from the oppressive heat, drinking from the cool, refreshing water. It's not hard to imagine that Jonas would have done the same!

—*Sam and Amy Miller*

Dedication

FIRST OF ALL, we dedicate this book to God, the one who has blessed us with an abundance of food, friends and family to enjoy. We also want to dedicate it to our mothers who are such wonderful cooks and who took the time to teach us the art of cooking.

Acknowledgments

GRATEFUL ACKNOWLEDGMENTS to our Miller and Coblentz families for allowing their time-honored recipes to be reduced and kitchen-tested, tasted and finally compiled in a book.

A Note From Rhoda

I ENJOYED helping Sam and Amy with this project, but I must admit I had no idea how much work is involved with compiling a cookbook! I count baking as a hobby and always anticipate trying out new recipes. A special thanks to my mom for teaching me the art of cooking and baking since I was eight years old. I hope this book will inspire you to try these recipes and find favorites among our collection.

A Note from Sam and Amy

WE TRIED OUR BEST to size these recipes for two people, but we also realize that not all appetites are created equal. Feel free to tweak these recipes to suit your own needs. If that means writing in the margins—by all means, do so!

Memorable Meals

I WILL VENTURE TO SAY that most of the meals that we could label as memorable, very likely have less to do with food than who they were eaten with or how they were served. In Bible times, serving a meal to a guest was considered a special act of hospitality and a token of friendship. Taking bread and salt together was sacred enough to be used as the confirmation of a covenant of peace between two parties. Even today we still consider food as something special to be shared with family and friends. Let me tell you about two meals in particular that stand out in my mind.

It was on an Easter Sunday, awash in sunshine and all the promises of spring, when Amy and I packed a picnic lunch and went for a stroll on the overgrown acres of a neighboring farm. This place was a real wilderness. The thorns and the brambles grew so thickly in places as to be almost impenetrable, but it was an awesome place to be in the springtime! Following a path up the hillside through a maze of trees and bushes, we made our way toward the long-neglected apple orchard and its delicious smelling blossoms. Close by the orchard, beneath some trees, we found a patch of grass dappled by sunshine and wildflowers with a grand view of the pastoral valley below. Here we spread our blanket and enjoyed our picnic lunch and the pleasure of each other's companionship.

Another time, we were in a Central American country when we stopped in to visit Delfina and Oscar, friends of my brother. They invited us to stay for lunch but we had other plans, so we said, "No, we can't stay." They insisted so we finally gave in and stayed.

Delfina fried some fish in their dirt-floor kitchen over a wood-fired oven while her four girls ran here and there, washing dishes, shoving a piece of wood into the fire, buying tortillas and getting whatever else was necessary for our lunch. It gave us an interesting view of daily Central American life. I don't generally eat fish that stare up at me from my plate, but those were served whole and they were surprisingly good. Rice, tortillas and an orange drink completed the meal. Amy said it was the best local food she had on our whole trip. While we ate, Oscar kept the flies away from us with a small hand fan. We were treated like honored guests and we felt that way, too!

—*Sam*

Contents

Appetizers, Beverages Dips and Miscellaneous

Having a sweet tooth is only natural for a small child and it seems that grandparents know just how to fulfill that craving. One of the most distinct memories that I have of visiting Grandma and Grandpa Miller is of their candy drawer. Of course the highlight of the visit came just before we left for home when Grandpa would carry me over to the cupboard, open the drawer and ask in his gentle voice, "Now, what kind would you like?"

He had a selection to make a child's eyes become the size and shape of saucers, but I always picked those round, pink peppermint candies. I used to call it *Doddy* (Grandpa) candy. Grandpa has passed on now and I always recall that particular memory when I think of him.

—*Rhoda*

Quick Banana Malt

2 ripe bananas, frozen*
6 Tbsp. chocolate milk powder
1½ c. milk

Slice bananas; puree with remaining ingredients in blender. Serve immediately. *To freeze bananas, peel and freeze overnight in an airtight plastic bag.

Orange Jewlet

6 oz. orange juice concentrate
¼ c. white sugar
1 c. milk
1 c. water
½ tsp. vanilla
10 ice cubes

Crush in blender until slushy. Serve immediately.

Party Punch

1 pkg. cherry Kool-Aid
1 pkg. strawberry Kool-Aid
6 oz. frozen orange juice
1-2 c. white sugar
3 qt. water
6 oz. frozen lemonade
7-Up

Mix first six ingredients together. Add ice and 7-Up when ready to serve.

Cranberry Punch

1 c. cranberry juice
1 c. pineapple juice
½ c. white sugar
¾ tsp. almond extract
2 c. ginger ale

Combine cranberry juice, pineapple juice, sugar and almond extract. Stir until sugar is dissolved; chill. Add ginger ale just before serving.

Appetizers, Beverages, Dips and Misc.

Hot Mulled Cider

⅛ c. brown sugar
⅛ tsp. salt
1 qt. cider
½ tsp. allspice
½ tsp. whole cloves
2 cinnamon sticks
dash nutmeg

Combine brown sugar, salt and cider. Pour into saucepan. Tie spices into a small piece of cheesecloth; add to cider mixture. Simmer uncovered for 20 minutes. Remove spices. Serve hot and use cinnamon sticks as muddlers.

Instant Hot Chocolate

4 c. powdered milk
1¼ c. powdered chocolate
  drink mix
½ c. powdered nondairy creamer
½ c. powdered sugar

Mix all ingredients and store in an airtight container. To serve, add ¼ c. mix to 1 c. boiling water.

Instant Spice Tea

¼ c. Lipton instant tea mix
1¼ c. white sugar
½ tsp. ground cinnamon
½ tsp. cloves
3½ oz. Tang
¾ pkg. lemon Kool-Aid

Mix all ingredients together. Store in an airtight container. To make tea, add 2 tsp. mix to 1 c. boiling water.

Frosty Fruit Drink

½ c. unsweetened raspberries
¾ c. frozen vanilla yogurt
1 ripe banana
¾ c. raspberry blend juice, chilled

In a blender combine all ingredients. Cover and process until smooth. Serve immediately.

Lemonade

2 lemons
2 limes
2 oranges
1 qt. water
1 c. white sugar

Save two thin slices from each of the fruits. Juice the remaining fruit. Pour into pitcher. Add water and sugar. Stir well. Store in refrigerator. Serve with ice and remaining fruit slices.

Strawberry Orange Shakes

1 c. orange juice (not concentrate)
¼ c. milk
1 c. frozen, sliced strawberries
1-2 tsp. white sugar
½ c. ice cubes

In a blender combine orange juice, milk, strawberries and sugar. Cover and process until smooth. Add ice cubes. Process until mixture reaches desired consistency. Pour into glasses. Garnish with a strawberry, orange wedge or mint sprig if desired. Serve immediately.

Cappuccino Mix

2 c. nondairy coffee creamer
1¼ c. nonfat dry milk
1 c. white sugar
⅓ c. cocoa mix
½ c. instant coffee
¼ c. powdered sugar
dash salt
⅓ c. instant vanilla pudding
½ lb. French vanilla cappuccino
¼ c. chocolate drink mix

Mix in a large bowl. To serve, mix 3 heaping tsp. to 1 c. boiling water.

Vintage Cooler

2 c. grape juice
1 c. raspberry sherbet
7-Up or Sprite

Beat together until sherbet is foamy.
Add 7-Up to suit your taste.

Lemonade Slush

⅔ c. lemonade concentrate,
    partially thawed
1 c. milk
⅔ c. water
½ tsp. vanilla extract
yellow food coloring, optional
10 ice cubes, crushed

In a blender, combine lemonade
concentrate, milk, water, vanilla and
food coloring. Cover and process until
blended. While processing, slowly add
crushed ice. Process until slushy. Serve
immediately.

Biscuit Bites

1 (12 oz.) tube refrigerated
    buttermilk biscuits
2 Tbsp. grated Parmesan cheese
1 tsp. onion powder

Cut each biscuit in half. Place on a
greased baking sheet. Combine
Parmesan cheese and onion powder.
Sprinkle over biscuits. Bake at 375° for
8-10 minutes or until golden brown.

Hamburger Cheese Dip

½ lb. hamburger, browned
½ tsp. chili powder
¼ tsp. garlic powder
4 oz. mild taco sauce
½ tsp. Worcestershire sauce
½ lb. Velveeta cheese

Mix together and heat. Serve with
nacho chips.

Tortilla Pinwheels

½ c. sour cream
1 oz. cream cheese, softened
¼ pkg. Ranch dressing mix
2 flour tortillas
broccoli, chopped
cauliflower, chopped
bacon, fried and crumbled
shredded cheese

Mix sour cream, cream cheese and dip mix. Spread over tortillas. Top with broccoli, cauliflower, crumbled bacon and shredded cheese. Roll up and chill for several hours. Slice ½" thick.

Pretzels with Cheese Dip

½ Tbsp. active dry yeast
½ c. warm warm (110°-115°)
1 Tbsp. butter
½ Tbsp. white sugar
¼ tsp. salt
1⅓ c. flour, divided

2 c. water
1 Tbsp. baking soda

Cheese Sauce:
4 oz. American cheese, cubed
1½ oz. cream cheese, cubed
1 Tbsp. milk

Dissolve yeast in warm water. Add butter, sugar, salt and 1 c. flour; beat until smooth. Add enough remaining flour to form a soft dough. Cover and let rise in a warm place for 20 minutes. Punch dough down. Divide into 6 equal pieces. On a floured board roll each piece into a 15" strip. Twist into a pretzel shape. In a large kettle, bring 2 c. water to a boil. Add baking soda. Drop 2 pretzels into water and boil for 1 minute. Remove and drain. Place on a greased baking sheet; sprinkle with coarse salt. Repeat for each pretzel. Bake at 475° for 10-12 minutes or until golden brown. Melt cheeses over medium heat; stir in milk. Serve with pretzels. Yield: 6 pretzels.

Appetizers, Beverages, Dips and Misc.

Mushroom Bacon Bites

6 med. fresh mushrooms
3 bacon strips, halved
¼ c. barbecue sauce

Wrap each mushroom with a piece of bacon; secure with toothpicks. Thread onto metal or soaked bamboo skewers. Brush with barbecue sauce. Grill uncovered over indirect medium heat for 10-15 minutes, or until bacon is crisp and mushrooms are tender, turning and basting occasionally with barbecue sauce.

Li'l Smokies

10 little smokies sausages
crescent rolls

Wrap small pieces of crescent roll dough around each smokie. Place on a greased baking sheet. Bake at 350° for 10-15 minutes or until golden brown.

Sausage Rolls

½ lb. bulk pork sausage
3 oz. cream cheese, cubed
1 tube crescent rolls

Cook sausage until browned; drain. Stir in cream cheese until melted. Separate crescent rolls into 4 rectangles. Seal seams. Spread rectangles with sausage mixture. Starting with long side, roll up jelly-roll style. Pinch seams and ends to seal. Place seam side down onto ungreased baking sheet. Bake at 350° for 20-25 minutes or until golden. Let set for 5 minutes before cutting into fourths.

Cheddar Bacon Toasts

½ c. shredded cheddar cheese
¼ c. mayonnaise
1½ Tbsp. fried, crumbled bacon
6 slices French bread

Combine cheese, mayonnaise and bacon. Spread on one side of the bread. Place on baking sheet and bake at 425° for 8-10 minutes or until golden brown.

Hanky Pankys

½ lb. hamburger
½ lb. sausage
½ lb. Velveeta cheese
½ Tbsp. oregano
¼ tsp. salt
½ Tbsp. Worcestershire sauce
¼ tsp. garlic powder
¼ tsp. pepper
½ loaf party rye bread

Brown hamburger and sausage together; drain. Add cheese and stir in to melt. Add next 5 ingredients. Spoon onto rye bread. Broil for 5 minutes. Can be frozen on baking sheets and stored in Ziplock bags. Keeps well in freezer.

Cheese Ball

8 oz. cream cheese, softened
1½ tsp. chopped onion
½ tsp. lemon juice
⅓ c. shredded cheddar cheese
1½ tsp. parsley
½ tsp. Worcestershire sauce
nuts

Mix first 6 ingredients together with fork. Form a ball and roll in nuts. Serve with any kind of crackers.

Ranch Pretzels

10 oz. small pretzel twists
½ pkg. Ranch dressing mix
¾ tsp. garlic powder
¾ tsp. dill weed
½ c. vegetable oil

Place pretzels in a bowl. Combine remaining ingredients and pour over pretzels. Stir to coat. Pour into a 9" x 13" baking pan. Bake at 200° for 1 hour, stirring every 15 minutes.

Appetizers, Beverages, Dips and Misc.

Spiced Pecans

1 egg white
1 tsp. cold water
4 c. pecan halves
½ c. white sugar
¼ tsp. salt
½ tsp. cinnamon

Beat egg white lightly. Add water; beat until frothy but not stiff. Add pecans; stir until well coated. Combine sugar, salt and cinnamon. Sprinkle over pecans. Toss to mix. Spread in a greased 10" x 15" baking pan. Bake at 250° for 45 minutes, stirring occasionally.

Mini Apple Pizzas

4 refrigerator biscuits
¼ c. brown sugar
1 Tbsp. flour
½ tsp. cinnamon
1 apple, peeled and shredded

Roll biscuits into 3½" circles. Place on lightly greased baking sheet. Combine sugar, flour and cinnamon. Mix well. Add apples. Spoon onto biscuits. Bake at 350° for 15-20 minutes. Serve warm.

Chewy Snack Squares

1¼ c. cornflakes
1 c. crisp rice cereal
¼ c. salted peanuts
¼ c. flaked coconut
¼ c. light corn syrup
¼ c. white sugar
2 Tbsp. butter
2 Tbsp. light cream

In a bowl combine cereal, peanuts and coconut. Set aside. Mix remaining ingredients together. Cook and stir over medium heat until the mixture reaches soft ball stage (240°). Pour over cereal mixture and toss to coat evenly. Pat into an 8" square pan. Cool before cutting.

[HINT]

Try using melted mint chocolate chips to make chocolate covered pretzels with a refreshing taste.

Oat Snack Mix

½ c. butter
⅓ c. honey
¼ c. brown sugar
1 tsp. cinnamon
½ tsp. salt
3 c. square oat cereal
1½ c. old-fashioned oats
1 c. chopped walnuts
½ c. chocolate-covered raisins

In a saucepan, combine butter, honey, sugar, cinnamon and salt. Heat and stir until sugar is dissolved. In a bowl combine cereal, oats and nuts. Drizzle with butter mixture and mix well. Place in a greased 10" x 15" pan. Bake uncovered at 275° for 45 minutes, stirring every 15 minutes. Cool for 15 minutes. Stir occasionally. Stir in chocolate-covered raisins. Store in airtight container.

Marshmallow Treats

⅓ c. butter
4½ c. mini marshmallows
5½ c. Rice Krispies

Grease a 9" x 13" pan with butter. Melt butter; add marshmallows. Stir until marshmallows are melted and mixture is well blended. Heat and stir for 2-3 minutes longer. Add Rice Krispies; mix well and pat into greased pan. Cut into squares.

Popcorn Scramble

6 c. popped corn, unsalted
2 c. Cheerios
2 c. peanuts, salted
2 c. Rice Chex squares
½ c. butter
¼ c. light Karo
1 c. brown sugar
½ tsp. soda
1 tsp. vanilla

Combine popcorn, Cheerios, peanuts and Rice Chex in a large bowl. Bring butter, Karo and brown sugar to a boil over low heat. Stir in soda and vanilla. Pour over dry mixture; stir until coated. Bake at 250° for 1 hour, stirring every 15 minutes.

Appetizers, Beverages, Dips and Misc.

Finger Jell-O

Layer 1:
⅔ c. blueberry Jell-O
1¼ c. water

Layer 2:
⅓ c. lemon Jell-O
½ c. + 2 Tbsp. water
½ c. sour cream
Cool Whip, for right consistency

Layer 3:
⅔ c. strawberry Jell-O
1¼ c. water

Peanut Butter Crispy Treats

1 c. white sugar
1 c. light Karo
1 c. creamy peanut butter
1 tsp. vanilla
6 c. Rice Krispies

Grease 9" x 13" pan with butter. Put sugar and Karo in pan. Cook, stirring constantly, until mixture boils. Remove from heat; add peanut butter and vanilla. Pour over cereal. Pat into greased pan. Cool and cut into squares.

Marshmallow Balls

½ pkg. mini colored
    marshmallows
1½ c. graham cracker crumbs
1 can sweetened condensed milk
coconut

Mix marshmallows and graham cracker crumbs. Add condensed milk. Drop by spoonfuls into coconut and form into balls. Place on waxed paper and let dry for 2 hours. Store in tightly covered container.

Caramel Corn

½ c. brown sugar
¼ c. butter
2 Tbsp. soda
⅛ tsp. salt
2 qt. popped corn

Bring sugar and butter to a boil. Boil gently for 4 minutes. Remove from heat and add soda and salt. Pour over popcorn. Stir. Put into a greased 9" x 13" pan. Bake at 200° for 45-60 minutes, stirring every 15 minutes.

Party Mix

½ c. butter
½ tsp. onion salt
½ tsp. garlic salt
½ tsp. seasoned salt
½ tsp. Worcestershire sauce
1 c. Cheerios
1 c. Rice Chex
1 c. Corn Chex
2 c. pretzels
1 c. peanuts
3 c. Lucky Charms

Mix all cereals except for Lucky Charms. Melt butter; add seasonings and Worcestershire sauce. Pour over mixed cereals, and toss until mixed. Bake at 200° for 1½ hours, stirring every 20 minutes. Add Lucky Charms after it has cooled. Store in airtight containers.

Garlic Cheese Bagel Spread

3 oz. cream cheese, softened
⅓ c. sour cream
2 garlic cloves, minced
½ tsp. basil
½ tsp. garlic power
½ tsp. oregano

Beat cream cheese until smooth. Add sour cream, garlic cloves and seasonings. Mix well. Toast bagels if desired and top with spread.

[H I N T]

Place pieces of leftover cubed fruit in an ice cube tray. Fill with water and freeze. These pretty cubes are a special addition to soda, iced tea or juice.

Appetizers, Beverages, Dips and Misc.

Cinnamon Spread

¼ c. butter, softened
¼ c. brown sugar
1 tsp. ground cinnamon
¼ tsp. ground nutmeg

Combine butter, sugar, cinnamon and nutmeg. Toast bagels if desired and top with spread.

Peachy Fruit Dip

1 c. fresh or canned peaches, sliced
3 oz. cream cheese, softened
¼ c. marshmallow créme

In a blender combine all ingredients. Cover and blend until smooth. Serve with fresh fruit.

Fruit Dip

½ can sweetened condensed milk
3 oz. frozen pink lemonade
3 c. Cool Whip

Mix and serve with fresh fruit.

Creamy Caramel Dip

3 oz. cream cheese, softened
½ c. brown sugar
½ c. sour cream
1 tsp. vanilla
1 tsp. ReaLemon
¼ c. instant vanilla pudding
½ c. milk

Beat cream cheese and sugar until smooth. Add sour cream, vanilla and ReaLemon; beat again. Mix pudding and milk and add to sour cream mixture. Serve with fresh fruit or angel food cubes.

[H I N T]

Many fudge recipes call for lining the pan with foil. To save time use foil baking pans instead. Just toss the pan away to save on clean up.

Creamy Fruit Dip

1 c. pineapple juice
¼ c. white sugar
1 Tbsp. clear jel
3 oz. cream cheese, softened
2 c. Cool Whip

Cook juice, sugar and clear jel until thickened. Cool. Add cream cheese and Cool Whip. Mix until creamy. Serve with fresh fruits of your choice.

Exotic Fruit Dip

3 oz. cream cheese, softened
1½ c. Cool Whip
½ c. peach or raspberry yogurt

Mix all ingredients until blended. Serve with fresh fruit.

Vegetable Dip

⅓ c. mayonnaise
⅓ c. sour cream
1½ tsp. dry onion flakes
1½ tsp. parsley flakes
½ tsp. dill weed
½ tsp. Ac'cent
1-2 drops Worcestershire sauce

Mix and chill. Serve with fresh vegetables.

Caramel Candy Apples

3 med. red apples
3 wooden skewers
¼ lb. light colored caramels
1 Tbsp. light cream

Wash and dry apples; stick skewers in stem end. Unwrap caramels and place in double boiler. Add cream. Cook until caramels are melted. Dip apples in syrup; twirl once or twice to cover evenly. Refrigerate for 2 hours.

Appetizers, Beverages, Dips and Misc.

Cream Cheese Mints

3 oz. cream
2½ c. powdered sugar
1-2 drops peppermint extract
food coloring of your choice

Blend ingredients thoroughly until it is the consistency of play dough. Roll into marble-sized balls, then roll in white sugar. Press into rubber mint molds. Unmold at once onto waxed paper.

Rocky Road Fudge

1 c. chocolate chips
¾ c. sweetened condensed milk
1 Tbsp. butter
1½ c. salted dry roasted peanuts
2 c. miniature marshmallows

In a saucepan combine the chocolate chips, milk and butter. Cook and stir over low heat until chips are melted and mixture is smooth. Remove from heat; stir in peanuts and marshmallows. Spread in a greased 8" square pan. Refrigerate until firm.

Fudge

1 c. white sugar
1 Tbsp. Karo
⅓ c. milk or cream
¾ Tbsp. cocoa
1 Tbsp. butter
½ tsp. vanilla
chopped nuts

Mix and boil sugar, Karo, milk and cocoa to a soft boil. Add butter and vanilla. Let set until cool. Beat until creamy; add nuts. Pour into greased dish.

Simple Caramels

2 c. brown sugar
1 c. light Karo
1 can sweetened condensed milk
1 c. butter

Boil for 12 minutes, stirring constantly. Pour into greased pan. Cool; cut and wrap.

Scotcharoos

½ c. Karo or honey
½ c. peanut butter
½ c. white sugar
3 c. Rice Krispies

Topping:
½ c. chocolate chips
½ c. butterscotch chips

Melt Karo or honey, peanut butter and white sugar over low heat. Stir in Rice Krispies. Press into an 8" square pan. Melt chocolate chips and butterscotch chips in double boiler. Spread on top of Rice Krispie mixture.

Twix Candy Bars

Club crackers
¼ c. brown sugar
¼ c. white sugar
¼ c. butter
2 Tbsp. milk
½ c. crushed graham crackers
½ c. chocolate chips
¼ c. butterscotch chips
¼ c. peanut butter

Line 8" square pan with Club crackers. Combine brown sugar, white sugar, butter and milk in saucepan. Simmer for 5 minutes. Add crushed graham crackers. Spread over Club crackers. Top with another layer of Club crackers. Melt chocolate chips, butterscotch chips and peanut butter. Spread on top of Club crackers. Cool and cut into squares. Taste like Twix candy bars.

Chocolate Cheese Fudge

½ lb. milk chocolate
3 oz. cream cheese
½ c. chopped walnuts

Melt chocolate in double boiler. Remove from heat and beat in cream cheese until smooth and shiny. Add nuts. Spread into a greased loaf pan. Cut into squares when set.

Butterscotch Bonbons

6 oz. butterscotch chips
½ c. peanut butter
1 c. mini marshmallows
1½ c. cornflakes

Melt butterscotch chips and peanut butter in double boiler. Remove from heat; add marshmallows and cornflakes. Toss to mix. Drop by teaspoonful onto waxed paper. Chill.

[H I N T]

When making s'mores, try using peanut butter cups instead of chocolate bars for a different flavor.

[H I N T]

Ice cubes made from lemonade will give your iced tea an added punch.

Breakfasts

I ride my bike to work. It's not necessarily the easiest way to commute—especially if it's raining cats and dogs or those times when the north wind is howling and the temperatures are subzero. But I can tell you this, I'm wide awake by the time I get to work!

I've found that biking helps me avoid one of those (almost) inevitables of getting married—that spare tire that slowly but surely would like to inflate just south of my chest. Over the course of a year I manage to rack up anywhere from 1,500 to 2,000 miles on my two-wheeler. I wonder how many burned calories that represents.

Speaking of calories, biking is also a great way to whet my appetite for one of Amy's delicious home-cooked meals when I get home in the evening. I only hope I lose more calories than I gain by that.

—*Sam*

Breakfast Pizza

½ tube crescent rolls
½ c. sausage crumbles
½ c. hash browns
onions
2 scrambled eggs, mixed with
　¼ c. milk
½ c. shredded cheddar cheese
salt to taste
pepper to taste

Press crescent rolls in a greased 8"
square pan. Top with sausage crumbles,
hash browns, onions, eggs and cheese.
Bake at 350° for 20 minutes or until
crust is golden brown.

Morning Mix-Up

1 c. frozen hash browns
½ c. cooked ham, diced
¼ c. onion, diced
1 Tbsp. cooking oil
3 eggs
salt and pepper
½ c. shredded cheddar cheese

Sauté potatoes, ham and onions in oil
for 10 minutes or until potatoes
are tender. Beat eggs, salt and pepper.
Add to skillet. Cook, stirring
occasionally, until eggs are set. Remove
from heat and gently stir in cheese.

Bacon and Egg Quiche

2 eggs
¾ c. milk
¼ c. Bisquick
2 Tbsp. butter, melted
4 strips bacon,
　fried and crumbled
½ c. cheddar cheese

Mix eggs, milk, Bisquick and butter.
Pour into greased 8" pie pan. Sprinkle
with bacon and cheese. Bake at 350° for
30 minutes or until knife comes out
clean.

Breakfast

Ham and Cheese Strata

5 slices bread
½ c. cooked ham or bacon
4 oz. American or cheddar cheese
2 eggs, slightly beaten
1⅓ c. milk

Arrange 2½ slices of bread on bottom of greased 8" square baking dish. Top with ¼ c. ham or bacon and half of cheese. Top with rest of bread; sprinkle remaining meat and cheese on bread. Mix eggs and milk; pour over everything. Refrigerate overnight. Bake at 350° for 45-60 minutes. Cut in squares and serve.

Breakfast Casserole

3 c. shredded hash browns
¾ c. shredded
   Monterey Jack cheese
1 c. diced, cooked ham
4 eggs
1 can evaporated milk
¼ tsp. pepper
⅛ tsp. salt

Place potatoes in 8" square baking dish. Sprinkle with cheese and ham. Beat eggs, milk, pepper and salt. Pour over potatoes. Cover and refrigerate for 30 minutes before baking. Bake uncovered at 350° for 55-60 minutes or until knife inserted in center comes out clean.

Breakfast Stack

hash browns, fried
eggs, scrambled
bacon, fried and crumbled
cheese sauce
peppers, chopped
fresh mushrooms, sliced
sour cream
onion, chopped

Layer in order given. Serve with muffins and orange juice.

Breakfast Burritos

1 c. hash browns
3 eggs
2 tsp. onions, chopped
2 tsp. green peppers, chopped
1½ c. browned sausage
4 (10") flour tortillas, warmed
¾ c. shredded cheddar cheese
salsa, optional
sour cream, optional

Fry hash browns according to package directions; set aside. Beat eggs; add onions and peppers. Cook and stir until eggs are set. Remove from heat. Add hash browns and sausage. Stir gently. Place approximately ¾ c. of filling on each tortilla; top with cheese. Roll up and place on greased baking sheet. Bake at 350° for 15-20 minutes or until heated thoroughly. Serve with salsa and sour cream.

Bacon Breakfast Pizza

1 c. Bisquick
¼ c. water
1½ c. sausage gravy
3 eggs
2 Tbsp. milk
½ lb. bacon, fried and crumbled
Velveeta cheese
3 potatoes, cubed

Mix Bisquick with water and press into 8" square baking dish. Bake at 350° for approximately 15 minutes or until golden brown. Pour ¾ c. sausage gravy over crust. Scramble eggs with milk. Pour over sausage gravy. Sprinkle bacon over eggs and top with cheese. Fry and season potatoes and spread over cheese. Top with remaining sausage gravy.

Layered Breakfast Casserole

Tater Tots
fried sausage
scrambled eggs, fried
cheese sauce
tortillas
sour cream and mushroom soup
pizza blend cheese

Layer ingredients in order given in baking dish. Bake at 325° until thoroughly heated.

Breakfast Skillet Meal

1 c. shredded potatoes
2 Tbsp. chopped onions
6 eggs
2 Tbsp. milk
¾ c. bacon, ham or sausage
salt
pepper
Velveeta cheese

In a large skillet, fry potatoes and onions in butter until tender. In a bowl beat together eggs and milk. Pour over potatoes. Sprinkle with meat. Season with salt and pepper. When eggs are set, top with cheese. Melt. Delicious served with toast and orange juice.

Blueberry Sour Cream Pancakes

1 c. flour
2 Tbsp. white sugar
2 tsp. baking powder
¼ tsp. salt
1 egg
¾ c. milk
½ c. sour cream
½ c. fresh or frozen blueberries

Combine dry ingredients. Beat egg; add milk and sour cream. Stir into dry ingredients, just until blended. Fold in the blueberries. Pour batter onto hot, greased griddle. Turn when bubbles form on top of pancakes. Serve with warm blueberry pie filling or regular syrup. Yield: 10 pancakes.

Cinnamon Breakfast Bites

¾ c. flour
½ c. crisp rice cereal, crushed
1 Tbsp. white sugar
1½ tsp. baking powder
¼ tsp. salt
2 Tbsp. butter flavored Crisco
¼ c. milk
½ tsp. cinnamon
¼ c. white sugar
2 Tbsp. butter, melted

Combine flour, cereal, 1 Tbsp. sugar, baking powder and salt. Cut in shortening until crumbly. Stir in milk just until moistened. Shape into 1" balls. Combine cinnamon and remaining sugar. Dip balls into butter, then in sugar and cinnamon mixture. Arrange in a single layer in a baking pan. Bake at 425° for 15-18 minutes, until a toothpick comes out clean.

Fluffy Pancakes

1½ c. flour
¾ tsp. salt
2 tsp. baking powder
1 Tbsp. white sugar
1 egg, separated
1½ c. milk

Stir dry ingredients together; add egg yolk and milk. Fold in beaten egg white. Bake on hot, greased griddle until golden brown.

Featherlight Pancakes

1 c. sifted flour
½ tsp. baking soda
¼ tsp. salt
1½ Tbsp. sugar
1 egg, separated
2 Tbsp. vinegar
¾ c. milk

Mix dry ingredients. Beat egg yolk, vinegar and milk. Stir into dry ingredients. Fold in beaten egg white. Bake on hot, greased griddle.

Our Favorite Pancakes

1 c. flour
1 Tbsp. white sugar
pinch of salt
1 tsp. baking powder
1 egg, separated
1 c. milk

Mix flour, sugar, salt and baking powder together. Beat egg yolk with milk, then add to flour mixture. Beat egg white until stiff and fold in last. Bake on hot, greased griddle until golden brown. Delicious.

French Toast

½ c. milk
2 eggs, slightly beaten
4 slices day-old bread

Combine milk, eggs and pinch of salt. Dip day-old bread into milk/egg mixture. This is enough for about 4 slices of bread. Fry in small amount of butter until golden brown. Serve hot with pancake syrup.

Breakfast

Cinnamon Toast

bread
butter
cinnamon
sugar

Toast bread. Butter while hot; sprinkle with mixture of 1 part cinnamon to 4 parts sugar. Keep warm in oven until serving time. Can keep cinnamon/sugar in a large shaker, then it's ready to use when needed.

Cinnamon Spice French Toast

2 eggs
½ c. milk
1 tsp. white sugar
¾ tsp. cinnamon
¼ tsp. nutmeg
4 slices wheat or white bread

Beat eggs, milk, sugar, cinnamon and nutmeg. Add bread, one slice at a time, and soak both sides. Melt butter in a griddle over medium heat. Fry bread on both sides until golden brown. Serve with syrup.

Hearty Breakfast Rolls

8 oz. can crescent rolls
2 Tbsp. strawberry jam or jelly
6 slices ham, thinly sliced
¾ c. Velveeta cheese or process cheese spread

Unroll crescent rolls into two rectangles; firmly press perforations together to seal. Spread rectangles with jam; top with ham and process cheese spread. Roll up each rectangle, starting at narrow end; seal edge. Cut each roll into four slices. Place, cut side down, in a greased 8" pie plate or round cake pan. Bake at 350° for 25-30 minutes.

Blueberry Brunch Bake

½ loaf French bread,
  cut into ½" cubes
¾ c. blueberries
6 oz. cream cheese, softened
4 eggs
¼ c. plain yogurt
¼ c. sour cream
½ tsp. vanilla
¼ tsp. cinnamon
¼ c. milk
¼ c. maple syrup

Place half of the bread cubes into a greased 8" square baking pan. Sprinkle with blueberries. Beat cream cheese until smooth. Beat in eggs, yogurt, sour cream, vanilla and cinnamon. Gradually add milk and syrup until blended. Pour half over the bread. Top with remaining bread and cream cheese mixture. Cover and refrigerate overnight. Remove from refrigerator 30 minutes before baking. Cover and bake at 350° for 30 minutes. Uncover; bake 15-20 minutes longer, until knife inserted in center comes out clean. Serve with additional blueberries and syrup.

Granola

3 c. rolled oats
1 c. wheat germ
½ c. coconut
½ c. chopped nuts
½ c. vegetable oil
½ c. honey
2 tsp. vanilla

Mix dry ingredients. Combine oil, honey and vanilla. Pour over oat mixture and stir. Bake at 275° for 1 hour, stirring every 15 minutes.

[HINT]

Wrap leftover pancakes or waffles in foil and freeze. On busy mornings, heat in your oven or microwave. (Be sure to remove foil before putting into microwave.)

Granola Mix

3 c. rolled oats
½ c. wheat germ
½ c. chopped nuts
½ c. coconut
½ c. butter
2 Tbsp. honey
2 Tbsp. molasses
½ c. brown sugar
½ tsp. vanilla
½ tsp. cinnamon
½ tsp. salt

Mix rolled oats, wheat germ, nuts and coconut until combined. Melt remaining ingredients together. Stir into dry ingredients until well coated. Spread thin layers on baking sheets and toast at 250° for 1 hour, stirring every 10-15 minutes. Cool and store in an airtight container.

Granola Cereal

2 Tbsp. vegetable oil
½ c. butter
¼ c. honey
⅛ tsp. salt
1 tsp. vanilla
3 c. oatmeal
1 c. coconut
¼ c. wheat germ

Mix and heat oil, butter, honey, salt and vanilla until butter is melted. Pour over oatmeal mixture and blend. Bake at 250° until golden brown, stirring every 20 minutes.

[H I N T]

Sloppy Joe Stretcher—Next time you have leftover sloppy joe meat, make an omelet. Spread some reheated meat inside and sprinkle with cheddar cheese. Fold and enjoy.

Breads, Biscuits and Muffins

The story is told of a young, newlywed lady who decided to try her hand at bread baking. She mixed the ingredients together, then set the dough aside to rise. It soon became apparent that not all was well. She had forgotten to put in the yeast! So she chucked the dough over the fence into the neighbors' pasture field. Later, looking out the window, she saw a rather humorous sight. The neighbors' horse was vigorously nodding his head up and down, trying to rid himself of a gob of stringy dough dangling from his mouth!

—*Sam*

Our Daily Bread

4 tsp. salt
⅓ c. molasses
1 egg
2¼ c. warm water
4 tsp. brown sugar
⅓ c. vegetable oil or melted lard
1 heaping Tbsp. yeast
¾ c. warm water
1 tsp. white sugar
¾ c. whole wheat flour
white bread flour

Mix salt, molasses, egg, 2¼ c. water, brown sugar and oil together in large bowl. In a small bowl mix together yeast, ¾ c. water and white sugar. Let rise. Add ¾ c. whole wheat flour and 1 c. white bread flour to large bowl ingredients. When yeast mixture has risen, add it to large bowl. Add more white bread flour to dough until right consistency, fairly stiff. Cover and let rise for 15 minutes and punch down. Cover and let rise for 30 minutes; punch down. Cover again and let rise for 1 hour. Form into 4 loaves, approximately 1¼ lbs. each. Let rise. Bake at 375° for 25 minutes. Remove from oven and butter tops.

Homemade Wheat Bread

½ c. honey
1 c. boiling water
1 Tbsp. salt
1 Tbsp. dough enhancer or
    wheat gluten
2 c. cold water
¾ c. vegetable oil or olive oil
2 Tbsp. yeast
2 c. wheat flour
6 c. bread flour

Stir honey into boiling water until well mixed; add salt and dough enhancer. Stir in cold water; add ½ c. oil. Sprinkle yeast on top. Let set until foamy. Knead in the flour until stiff dough forms. Add ¼ c. oil last. Let rise until double; punch down. Let rise again. Divide into 4 loaves, 1¼ lb. each. Let rise in pans until double in size. Bake at 350° for 25 minutes or until golden brown.

Melt-in-Your-Mouth Dinner Rolls

½ Tbsp. yeast
¼ c. warm water
½ Tbsp. white sugar
½ tsp. baking powder
½ c. milk
2½ Tbsp. butter
¼ c. white sugar
dash of salt
1 egg, beaten
2¼ c. bread flour

Dissolve yeast in warm water; add ½ Tbsp. sugar and baking powder. Let set for 20 minutes. Scald milk, butter, ¼ c. sugar and salt. Cool, then add the egg. Add to yeast mixture. Mix in flour. Cover and refrigerate overnight. Roll out and shape as butterhorns. Let rise until double. Bake at 400° for 10-15 minutes. Brush with melted butter.

Tennessee Pumpkin Bread

⅓ c. shortening
1⅓ c. white sugar
½ tsp. vanilla
2 eggs
1 c. pumpkin
1⅔ c. flour
¼ tsp. baking powder
1 tsp. baking soda
¾ tsp. salt
½ tsp. cinnamon
½ tsp. nutmeg
⅓ c. water
½ c. nuts, optional

In a bowl cream shortening, sugar and vanilla. Beat in eggs. Stir in pumpkin and add dry ingredients in 4 additions, alternately with water, just until smooth. Do not overbeat. Fold in nuts. Pour into a greased bread pan. Bake at 350° for approximately 65 minutes. Let cool in pan for about 15 minutes. Then take out and put on a rack to cool.

[**H I N T**]

It's easy to serve molded pats of butter with rolls on a buffet. Soften the butter and press into candy molds. Chill in refrigerator; invert onto a dish. These pretty pats are very little fuss.

Pumpkin Bread

2 eggs
½ c. vegetable oil
⅓ c. water
1 c. pumpkin
1½ c. white sugar
1½ c. flour
1 tsp. baking soda
¾ tsp. salt
1½ tsp. nutmeg
1½ tsp. cinnamon
¼ tsp. ginger

Beat eggs; add oil, water and pumpkin. Mix well, then add rest of ingredients. Bake in a greased loaf pan at 350° for 50-60 minutes or until toothpick comes out clean. You may add chopped nuts or chocolate chips.

Banana Nut Bread

1 pkg. yellow cake mix
1 egg
½ c. milk
1 c. mashed ripe bananas
½ c. chopped pecans

Combine cake mix, egg and milk. Add bananas; beat on medium speed for 2 minutes. Stir in pecans. Pour into 2 greased 8" x 4" x 2" loaf pans. Bake at 350° for 40-45 minutes, until toothpick comes out clean. These freeze well.

Banana Bread

1 egg
½ c. mashed ripe bananas
¼ c. vegetable oil
2 Tbsp. buttermilk
¾ c. white sugar
½ tsp. vanilla
1 c. flour
½ tsp. baking soda
¼ tsp. salt
½ c. chopped nuts

Combine egg, bananas, vegetable oil, buttermilk, sugar and vanilla. Add flour, soda and salt. Mix just until blended. Fold in nuts. Pour into greased loaf pan. Bake at 325° for 45-50 minutes or until toothpick comes out clean.

Parmesan Garlic Bread

2 Tbsp. butter, softened
2 Tbsp. vegetable oil
2 Tbsp. grated Parmesan cheese
½ tsp. garlic powder
¼ tsp. parsley
¼ tsp. lemon pepper
4 thick slices homemade or
  French bread

Mix butter, oil and cheese. Add garlic powder, parsley and lemon pepper. Mix until smooth. Spread mixture evenly on both sides of the bread. Place on baking sheet. Cover with foil. Bake at 400° for 15-20 minutes. Serve warm.

Pizza Bread

1 loaf frozen white bread dough,
  thawed
mozzarella cheese
pizza seasonings
pepperoni
mushrooms
onions
green peppers

Roll out dough 6" x 16". Layer with remaining ingredients in order given. Roll up dough and pinch edges to seal. Bake at 375° for 15-20 minutes or until golden brown.

Cheesy Texas Toast

1 Tbsp. butter, softened
2 slices French bread
¼ tsp. garlic powder
½ c. shredded mozzarella cheese

Spread butter on one side of each slice of bread; sprinkle with garlic powder and cheese. Bake at 400° for 5-7 minutes on an ungreased baking sheet.

Basil Buttered French Bread

1 Tbsp. butter, softened
¼ tsp. dried basil
2 slices French bread

Combine butter and basil. Brush over one side of each bread slice. Place buttered side up on an ungreased baking sheet. Bake at 400° for 5 minutes or until golden brown.

Quick and Easy Pizza Dough

1 Tbsp. yeast
1 tsp. white sugar
1 c. warm water
2 Tbsp. vegetable oil
1 tsp. salt
2½ c. Thesco flour

Dissolve yeast and sugar in water. Stir in remaining ingredients and beat vigorously. Let rise for 5 minutes. Roll out dough and place in greased pizza pan. Let set for 30 minutes, then add toppings. Bake at 375° for 25 minutes or until done.

Easy Pizza Dough

¾ tsp. yeast
¼ c. warm water
¼ tsp. white sugar
⅓ tsp. salt
1 Tbsp. vegetable oil
¾ c. flour

Dissolve yeast in water; add sugar, salt and oil. Add half of flour and beat. Add remaining flour and knead for 5 minutes. Pat into a greased 7" x 11" or 9" x 9" pan. Add pizza toppings and bake at 350° for 20-25 minutes.

Country Biscuits

1 c. flour
1½ tsp. baking powder
½ tsp. salt
¼ c. shortening
⅓ c. milk

Combine flour, baking powder and salt. Cut in shortening until crumbly. Add milk. Form into a ball. Transfer to a lightly floured surface. Knead gently. Roll out dough to a ½" thickness. Cut with 2" biscuit cutter. Place on ungreased baking sheet. Bake at 425° for 12-14 minutes or until golden. Do not overbake. Yield: approx. 6 biscuits.

[H I N T]

To give pancakes an extra special flavor, add some ground cinnamon and vanilla to the batter.

Breads, Biscuits and Muffins

Buttermilk Biscuits

1 c. flour
⅛ tsp. baking soda
1⅛ tsp. baking powder
½ tsp. salt
3 Tbsp. shortening
½ c. buttermilk

Combine dry ingredients. Cut in shortening until crumbly. Add buttermilk. Drop by teaspoonful onto greased baking sheet. Bake at 450° for 12-15 minutes.

Melt-in-Your-Mouth Biscuits

2 c. flour
2 Tbsp. white sugar
2 tsp. baking powder
½ tsp. cream of tartar
½ tsp. salt
½ c. shortening
⅔ c. milk
1 egg, unbeaten

Mix dry ingredients together and cut in shortening until crumbly. Pour in milk slowly, mixing well after each addition. Add egg; stir well. Drop by tablespoonful onto greased baking sheet. Bake at 450° for 10-15 minutes. Yield: 9-12 biscuits.

Monkey Bread

1 tube buttermilk biscuits
1 Tbsp. cinnamon
2 Tbsp. white sugar
chopped nuts, optional

Sauce:
2 Tbsp. butter, melted
1 tsp. light Karo
⅓ c. brown sugar

Cut each biscuit in 4 pieces. Combine cinnamon and sugar. Roll each biscuit piece in the mixture. Sprinkle nuts in greased 8" square baking dish. Layer biscuit pieces on top. Combine sauce ingredients and bring to a boil. Remove from heat and pour over biscuits in pan. Bake at 350° for 15 minutes or until biscuits are baked. Invert immediately.

Sour Cream Rolls

1½ tsp. yeast
2 Tbsp. warm water
2 Tbsp. white sugar
¼ tsp. salt
¼ c. sour cream
3 Tbsp. butter, melted
1 egg, beaten
1½ c. flour

2 tsp. butter, melted
½ c. brown sugar
¼ tsp. cinnamon

Glaze:
⅓ c. brown sugar
¼ c. sour cream
2 Tbsp. butter, melted
1½ tsp. milk

Dissolve yeast in the warm water. Add sugar, salt, sour cream, butter and egg. Gradually add flour to form stiff dough. Cover and let rise in warm place until double in size. Turn dough onto floured surface and knead 15 times. Roll out in a 12" circle. Brush with melted butter. Mix together brown sugar and cinnamon. Sprinkle evenly over dough. Cut into 10 pie-shaped pieces. Roll up, starting with wide end. Place point side down in a greased 8" or 9" baking dish. Cover; let rise. Bake at 350° for 20-25 minutes. Bring glaze ingredients to a boil and cook for 3 minutes; pour over hot rolls.

Cinnamon Rolls

½ c. milk, scalded
¼ c. white sugar
¾ tsp. salt
¼ c. shortening
2 tsp. yeast
½ c. lukewarm water
1 egg, beaten
2½ c. flour

butter
brown sugar
cinnamon

Pour milk over sugar, salt and shortening. Dissolve yeast in warm water. When milk has cooled, add yeast mixture and beaten egg. Beat well. Add flour gradually, beating well. Place in greased bowl. Let rise until double. Roll out and spread with butter, sugar and cinnamon. Roll up jelly-roll style and cut. Place in a greased baking pan. Let rise again, then bake at 350° for 15-20 minutes or until lightly browned. Frost with caramel icing.

Blueberry Sour Cream Streusel Muffins

1 c. flour
1 tsp. baking powder
¼ tsp. baking soda
¼ tsp. salt
1½ tsp. white sugar
1 sm. egg, beaten
½ c. sour cream
2 Tbsp. milk
2 Tbsp. vegetable oil
¾ c. blueberries

Streusel Topping:
¼ c. brown sugar
2 Tbsp. flour
½ tsp. cinnamon
1½ Tbsp. butter, softened

Sift flour with baking powder, soda, salt and sugar. Beat egg with sour cream, milk and oil. Stir only until blended. Carefully fold in blueberries. Spoon into greased muffin tins. Mix brown sugar with flour and cinnamon. Cut in butter until crumbly. Sprinkle over muffins. Bake at 425° for 15-20 minutes or until topping is golden brown and toothpick comes out clean. Yield: 6 muffins.

Featherlight Muffins

⅓ c. shortening
½ c. white sugar
1 egg
1½ c. flour
1½ tsp. baking powder
½ tsp. salt
½ c. milk

Topping:
½ c. butter, melted
½ c. white sugar
1 tsp. cinnamon

Cream shortening and sugar; add egg. Mix dry ingredients. Add slowly to creamed mixture along with milk. Fill greased muffin pans ⅔ full. Bake at 325° for 25 minutes or until toothpick comes out clean. Cool for 4 minutes. Roll in melted butter, then in sugar mixture.

Apple Streusel Muffins

1 c. flour
½ c. brown sugar
1½ tsp. baking powder
¾ tsp. cinnamon
¼ tsp. salt
¼ tsp. baking soda
1 egg, beaten
1 c. sour cream
2 Tbsp. butter, melted
¾ c. diced apples

Sift together flour, sugar, baking powder, cinnamon, salt and baking soda. Beat egg, sour cream and butter. Add all at once to dry ingredients along with apples. Stir just until moistened. Fill well-greased muffin tins ⅔ full. Combine topping ingredients until crumbly; sprinkle over batter. Bake at 400° for 20 minutes or until toothpick comes out clean.

Streusel Topping:
¼ c. brown sugar
1 Tbsp. flour
1 Tbsp. cold butter
2 Tbsp. chopped pecans, optional

Peanut Banana Muffins

¾ c. flour
¼ c. white sugar
½ tsp. baking powder
¼ tsp. baking soda
¼ tsp. salt
1 sm. egg
¼ c. butter, melted
¾ c. mashed ripe bananas
⅓ c. peanut butter chips

Combine flour, sugar, baking powder, soda and salt. Combine egg, butter and bananas. Stir into dry ingredients just until moistened. Fold in chips. Fill greased muffin cups ¾ full. Bake at 375° for 18-22 minutes or until toothpick comes out clean. Cool for 5 minutes before removing from pan to a wire rack.

Breads, Biscuits and Muffins

Oatmeal Honey Muffins

¾ c. quick-cooking oats
½ c. flour
2 Tbsp. brown sugar, packed
1½ tsp. baking powder
¼ tsp. salt
1 sm. egg
⅓ c. milk
2½ Tbsp. vegetable oil
2 Tbsp. honey
¼ c. raisins
¼ c. chopped walnuts

Combine oats, flour, brown sugar, baking powder and salt. In another bowl combine egg, milk, oil and honey. Sir into dry ingredients just until moistened. Fold in raisins and walnuts. Fill greased or paper-lined muffin cups ⅔ full. Bake at 400° for 15-18 minutes or until toothpick comes out clean.

Cappuccino Muffins

Espresso Spread:
4 oz. cream cheese, softened
½ tsp. instant coffee granules
1 Tbsp. white sugar
½ tsp. vanilla
¼ c. mini chocolate chips

Muffins:
2 c. flour
¾ c. white sugar
2½ tsp. baking powder
1 tsp. cinnamon
½ tsp. salt
1 c. milk
2 Tbsp. instant coffee granules
½ c. butter, melted
1 egg, beaten
1 tsp. vanilla
¾ c. mini chocolate chips

Combine the spread ingredients until well blended. Refrigerate until serving. Combine flour, sugar, baking powder, cinnamon and salt. In another bowl, stir milk and coffee granules until coffee is dissolved. Add butter, egg and vanilla; mix well. Stir into dry ingredients just until moistened. Add chocolate chips. Fill greased or paper-lined muffin cups ⅔ full. Bake at 375° for 17-20 minutes or until muffins test done. Cool for 5 minutes before removing muffins from pans to wire rack. Serve with espresso spread.

Fudgy Banana Muffins

2¼ c. flour
½ c. white sugar
1½ tsp. baking powder
1 tsp. baking soda
¼ tsp. salt
1¼ c. milk
1 egg
1 Tbsp. vegetable oil
3 ripe bananas, mashed
1 c. milk chocolate chips

Mix dry ingredients well. In separate bowl, mix milk, egg, oil and bananas. Stir into dry ingredients just until blended. Add chocolate chips. Fill muffin cups ⅔ full; bake at 350° for 15 minutes. These muffins freeze well.

Coffee Cake Muffins

¼ c. brown sugar
¼ c. chopped pecans
1 tsp. cinnamon
1½ c. flour
½ c. white sugar
2 tsp. baking powder
¼ tsp. baking soda
¼ tsp. salt
1 egg
¾ c. milk
⅓ c. vegetable oil

Glaze:
½ c. powdered sugar
1 tsp. vanilla
1 Tbsp. milk

Combine brown sugar, pecans and cinnamon; set aside. Mix flour, sugar, baking powder, soda and salt. In another bowl beat egg, milk and oil. Stir into dry ingredients just until moistened. Spoon 1 tablespoon of batter into paper-lined muffin cups. Top each with 1 teaspoon nut mixture and 2 Tbsp. batter. Top with remaining nut mixture. Bake at 400° for 22-24 minutes or until toothpick comes out clean. Cool for 10 minutes. Spoon glaze over muffins.

Breads, Biscuits and Muffins

Peanut Butter and Jelly Mini Muffins

½ c. flour
3 Tbsp. brown sugar
½ tsp. baking powder
¼ tsp. baking soda
⅛ tsp. salt
1 egg
¼ c. vanilla yogurt
1½ Tbsp. creamy peanut butter
1 Tbsp. vegetable oil
1½ Tbsp. grape or
    strawberry jelly

Combine flour, brown sugar, baking powder, soda and salt. In a small bowl, beat the egg, yogurt, peanut butter and oil. Stir into dry ingredients just until moistened. Fill paper-lined mini muffin cups half full. Top each with ¼ tsp. jelly and remaining batter. Bake at 400° for 10-12 minutes.

Cornmeal Muffins

½ c. cornmeal
½ c. flour
2 tsp. baking powder
¼ tsp. salt
1 Tbsp. brown sugar
1 beaten egg
½ c. milk
2 Tbsp. vegetable oil

Mix dry ingredients. Make a well and add liquids. Stir just until moistened. Pour into greased muffin tins. Bake at 375° until toothpick comes out clean.

[HINT]

To cut down on back and forth trips to the kitchen during a backyard picnic, use a six-cup muffin tin to hold ketchup, mustard, etc.

Main Dishes

A young acquaintance of mine decided to cook a beef roast one day for her husband with whom she had only recently exchanged the nuptial vows. Taking a package from the freezer, marked roast, she opened it and chucked it into a kettle to slow-cook until it was nice and tender. She did notice that the meat looked a little different from what she had expected, but then the package had said "roast" so why worry?

She simmered that "roast" for five long hours, and you can well imagine how proud she was of her cooking abilities when that juicy hunk of meat literally fell apart upon having a fork stuck into it. What an opportunity to impress upon hubby's mind once and for all that this woman can cook! Dinner was served and on the first bite, to her chagrin, the "roast" had its name changed to hamburger.

—*Sam*

Stuffed Baked Potatoes

2 lg. baking potatoes
2 Tbsp. butter
1 Tbsp. chives
⅔ c. cheddar cheese
3 bacon slices,
  fried and crumbled
salt and pepper to taste

Bake potatoes until tender and skins are very crisp—about 1¼ hours. Cut potatoes in half lengthwise and scoop out centers into a bowl. Add butter and mash until smooth; fold in chives, cheese, bacon, salt and pepper. Mound mixture back into potato shells and bake at 400° for another 15 minutes.

Crusty Baked Potatoes

3 med. potatoes
2 Tbsp. butter, melted
¾ c. saltine cracker crumbs
1½ tsp. seasoning salt

Pare potatoes. Wash and dry; cut into wedges. Roll in butter and then in cracker crumbs mixed with seasoning salt. Place in greased baking dish. Bake at 350° uncovered for 1 hour. Delicious served with sour cream.

Parsley Potatoes

4 med. potatoes
butter, melted
garlic powder
cheddar cheese
parsley

Cut potatoes into chunks. Cook until almost soft; put into baking dish. Drizzle with melted butter. Sprinkle with garlic powder and cheddar cheese. Garnish with parsley. Put in oven at 300° until cheese melts. Serve with sour cream.

[H I N T]

When freezing fish, put fish in a Ziplock bag. Fill bag with water, press out the air and seal. This prevents freezer burn.

Main Dishes

Patio Potatoes

3 med. potatoes, cooked and
 shoestring grated
1 c. sour cream
¼ tsp. salt
1 c. shredded cheddar cheese
¼ c. butter, melted
¼ c. chopped onion
⅛ tsp. pepper

Mix everything together and bake at 350° for 30-35 minutes or until lightly browned.

Holiday Potatoes

4 c. hot mashed potatoes
½ c. sour cream
4 oz. cream cheese, softened
4 Tbsp. butter, softened
1 egg, beaten
½ c. milk
salt to taste
dash of pepper

Mix all ingredients well. Place in greased casserole and refrigerate several hours or overnight. Bake at 350° for 35-40 minutes or until hot.

Baked Potato Spears

2 med. potatoes
6 Tbsp. Miracle Whip
onion salt
pepper

Dip:
¾ c. Miracle Whip
6 Tbsp. Parmesan cheese
6 Tbsp. milk
2 tsp. chives

Cut potatoes lengthwise into wedges. Brush with Miracle Whip and season with onion salt and pepper. Place on greased cookie sheet and bake at 375° for 50 minutes. Serve with dip.

Potato Cakes

leftover mashed potatoes
1 egg

Add egg to mashed potatoes; mix
well. Fry in butter or oil in a frying pan.
Drop in by heaping teaspoons.
Brown on each side. Delicious served
with ketchup.

Potluck Potatoes

1 lb. potatoes
¼ c. butter, melted
½ tsp. salt
⅛ tsp. pepper
¼ c. chopped onion
½ can cream of chicken soup
1 c. sour cream
1 c. diced Velveeta cheese
1 c. crushed cornflakes
2 Tbsp. butter, melted

Cook potatoes until tender; cool, then
cut up. Melt ¼ c. butter, salt, pepper,
onion, soup, sour cream and cheese.
Mix with potatoes. Top with cornflake
crumbs, mixed with 2 Tbsp. melted
butter. Bake at 350° for approximately
35 minutes or until hot.

Potluck Potatoes

1 lb. potatoes,
    cooked and shredded
⅔ c. sour cream
⅔ c. cubed Velveeta cheese
½ can cream of mushroom soup
⅓ tsp. onion salt
dash of pepper
⅓ tsp. seasoning salt
⅔ c. crushed cornflakes
⅓ stick butter, melted

In a saucepan, heat sour cream,
Velveeta cheese, soup, onion salt,
pepper and seasoning salt over
medium heat until cheese melts.
Mix sauce with potatoes; put in baking
dish. Bake at 350° for 45 minutes or
until hot. Sprinkle with crumbs made
with cornflakes and butter.

Souper Scalloped Potatoes

4 c. cooked, sliced potatoes
1 can cream of mushroom soup
½ c. milk or evaporated milk
¼ c. chopped onion
¼ tsp. pepper
½ tsp. salt
seasoning salt to taste

Layer in a baking dish. Bake uncovered at 375° for 30-45 minutes.

Idaho Tacos

2 med. baked potatoes
½ lb. hamburger
½ pkg. taco seasoning
⅓ c. water
½ c. shredded cheddar cheese
½ c. chopped green onions
salsa, optional

In a skillet brown hamburger; drain. Add taco seasoning and water; simmer 5 minutes. With a sharp knife, cut an x in the top of each potato. Fluff pulp with fork. Top with taco meat, cheese and onions. Serve with salsa.

Underground Ham Casserole

1 c. diced ham
2 Tbsp. chopped onions
1 Tbsp. butter
1 tsp. Worcestershire sauce
½ can cream of mushroom soup
½ c. Velveeta cheese
¼ c. milk
½ c. sour cream
salt to taste
1 qt. mashed potatoes
fried and crumbled bacon

In a saucepan fry ham and onions in butter. Add Worcestershire sauce, mushroom soup and cheese. Heat until cheese is melted. Put in bottom of casserole dish. Add milk, sour cream and salt to mashed potatoes; mix well. Put on top of ham mixture in dish and top with a few slices Velveeta cheese. Add bacon on top. Put in oven until heated thoroughly.

Chicken Potato Casserole

cooked, diced potatoes
2 boneless chicken breasts,
    fried and cut in small pieces
¼ c. butter
¾ c. cream of chicken soup
½ c. sour cream
½ c. Miracle Whip
¼ tsp. salt
½ c. Velveeta cheese, cubed

Grease an 8" square baking dish. Fill half full with potatoes. Place chicken pieces on top of potatoes. Melt butter; add soup, sour cream, Miracle Whip, salt and cheese. Heat until cheese is melted. Pour on top of chicken and stir to coat. You can add seasonings like garlic or onion salt if desired. Bake uncovered at 350° for 30-40 minutes, until heated through.

Shepherd's Pie

1 lb. hamburger, browned
    and seasoned
brown gravy
1¼ lb. potatoes, peeled,
    cooked and mashed
2 Tbsp. butter
1 egg, beaten
¼ c. milk
3 oz. cream cheese
¼ c. sour cream
salt to taste
Velveeta cheese

Stir hamburger into gravy. Add butter, egg, milk, cream cheese and sour cream to the potatoes. Put hamburger mixture in bottom of casserole. Pour mashed potatoes on top. Top with Velveeta cheese slices. Bake at 350° until hot and cheese is melted.

[H I N T]

When cooking on the grill, spray the grill rack with nonstick cooking spray before turning on the grill. This keeps food from sticking to the rack.

Main Dishes

Mashed Potato Casserole

½ lb. hamburger
¾ tsp. vinegar
½ c. cracker crumbs
1 egg, beaten
¼ lb. ground hot dogs
½ tsp. salt
¼ c. brown sugar
2 Tbsp. water
1¼ lb. potatoes, peeled, cooked
   and mashed
3 oz. cream cheese
¼ c. milk
¼ c. butter, softened
½ tsp. salt
¼ c. sour cream
1 egg, beaten
Velveeta cheese

Mix first 8 ingredients together and press into casserole dish. Bake at 350° until meat is no longer pink. Mix together remaining ingredients except cheese. Keep hot until meat is done. Pour on top of meat and place Velveeta cheese slices on potatoes. Bake until cheese melts.

Crunchy Ham and Potato Casserole

1 lb. hash browns, thawed
1 c. cubed ham
¾ c. shredded cheddar cheese
¼ c. butter
1 c. cream of chicken soup
1 c. sour cream
¼ tsp. pepper
¼ c. chopped onions
1 c. crushed cornflakes
2 Tbsp. butter, melted

Mix potatoes, ham and cheese. Melt butter; add soup, sour cream, pepper and onions. Add to potatoes. Mixture will be stiff. Bake at 350° for 30 minutes. Place cornflake crumbs made with cornflakes and butter on top of casserole. Bake another 20-25 minutes.

Mashed Potato Hamburger Pea Casserole

1 pt. peas
1 lb. hamburger
chopped onions
salt and pepper to taste
1 qt. hot mashed potatoes
Velveeta cheese

Cook peas and put in bottom of casserole dish. Brown hamburger; add chopped onions, salt and pepper. Add to peas. Add 1 qt. hot mashed potatoes to dish. Top with slices of Velveeta cheese. Bake until hot and cheese is melted.

Potato Stack Casserole

16 oz. hash browns
½ c. sour cream
½ c. milk
½ pkg. Ranch dressing mix
1 lb. hamburger
onions
green peppers
½ pkg. taco seasoning
2 Tbsp. butter
2 Tbsp. flour
1 c. milk
½ c. Velveeta cheese
½ tsp. salt
crushed Doritos

Fry hash browns; add salt and pepper. Mix sour cream, milk and Ranch dressing mix. Pour over potatoes. Fry hamburger; add onions and green peppers. Mix in taco seasoning. Combine potato and hamburger mix and put into baking dish. In saucepan melt butter; add flour when bubbles form. Add milk, Velveeta cheese and salt. Poke holes in potato hamburger mix and pour cheese sauce over this. Bake for 30 minutes. Before serving, top with crushed Doritos.

Quick Tater Tot Casserole

1 lb. hamburger
1 sm. onion, chopped
salt and pepper to taste
16 oz. frozen Tater Tots
1 can cream of mushroom soup
½ soup can milk
1 c. shredded cheddar cheese

In a skillet, brown the meat and onions. Drain any fat. Season with salt and pepper. Place in a 2 qt. casserole. Top with Tater Tots. Combine soup and milk and pour over potatoes. Sprinkle with cheese. Bake at 350° for 30-40 minutes.

Baked Hash Browns

4 frozen hash brown patties
½ tsp. salt
¼ tsp. garlic powder
½ c. whipping cream
⅓ c. shredded cheddar cheese

Place patties into a greased 8" square baking dish. Sprinkle with salt and garlic powder. Pour cream over patties. Bake uncovered at 350° for 50 minutes. Sprinkle with cheese. Bake for 5-10 minutes longer until cheese is melted.

Meat Potato Quiche

3 c. shredded raw potatoes
3 Tbsp. vegetable oil
1 c. grated Swiss or cheddar cheese
¼ c. chopped onions
¾ c. cooked, diced
    chicken or ham
2 eggs
1 can evaporated milk
½ tsp. salt
⅛ tsp. pepper

Preheat oven to 425°. Press potatoes mixed with oil into bottom and up sides of a 9" pie plate. Bake for 15 minutes. Place cheese, onion and meat on crust. Beat eggs, milk, salt and pepper. Pour over meat mixture. Bake for 30 minutes or until lightly browned.

Table for Two

[HINT]

Taco Meat Turnaround—Top pizza crust with a mixture of sour cream and refried beans. Sprinkle on leftover taco meat and bake until heated through. Serve with tomatoes, lettuce and cheese.

Porcupine Meatballs

¾ lb. hamburger
1½ slices bread, cubed
⅓ c. milk
1 egg, beaten
⅛ c. minute rice
½ tsp. salt
⅛ tsp. pepper
¼ c. chopped onion

Barbecue Sauce:
¼ c. tomato juice
¼ tsp. Worcestershire sauce
¼ tsp. chili powder
1 c. ketchup
¼ c. brown sugar

For meatballs, soak bread in milk; add beaten egg. Mix with hamburger and remaining ingredients. Shape into balls and place in single layer in baking dish. Mix sauce ingredients and pour over meatballs. Bake uncovered at 400° for 30 minutes. Cover and bake for 35 minutes longer at 350°.

Make-Ahead Meatballs

2 eggs
1 c. dry bread or cracker crumbs
1½ tsp. salt
¼ c. chopped onion
1 tsp. Worcestershire sauce
¼ tsp. pepper
2 lb. hamburger

Beat eggs; add everything except hamburger and stir. Add hamburger and mix well. Shape into small balls (1½"). Place in single layer on a baking sheet. Bake at 375° for 15-20 minutes or until no longer pink. Cool and place in freezer bags. Freeze for up to 3 months. You can use this recipe for Barbecue Meatballs and Sweet and Sour Meatballs.

Main Dishes

Barbecue Meatballs

10 meatballs, frozen or thawed
⅛ tsp. garlic powder
½ c. ketchup
½ c. brown sugar
⅛ tsp. liquid smoke

Place meatballs in a small ungreased baking dish. Combine sauce ingredients; pour over meatballs. Cover and bake at 350° for 45 minutes to 1 hour until hot.

Sweet and Sour Meatballs

1 c. pineapple chunks
¼ c. water
1½ Tbsp. vinegar
1½ tsp. soy sauce
¼ c. brown sugar
1½ Tbsp. clear jel
10 meatballs, frozen or thawed
½ green pepper, chopped
hot cooked rice

Drain pineapple, reserving juice. Set pineapple aside. Add water to juice if needed to measure ½ c.; pour into saucepan. Add ¼ c. water, vinegar, soy sauce and brown sugar. Bring to a boil; add clear jel which has been mixed with a little water. Cook until thick. Add pineapple, meatballs and peppers. Simmer uncovered for 20 minutes or until heated through. Serve over rice.

[H I N T]

*Rice Rerun—Warm up leftover rice and serve
with cheese sauce for an easy lunch.*

Tangy Barbecue Meatballs

1 lb. hamburger
⅓ c. oatmeal
1 sm. egg
4 oz. evaporated milk
⅓ c. cracker crumbs
⅛ tsp. garlic salt
⅛ tsp. pepper
2 Tbsp. chopped onion
⅔ tsp. salt
⅔ tsp. chili powder

Barbecue Sauce:
⅔ c. ketchup
⅓ c. brown sugar
⅛ tsp. garlic powder
1 Tbsp. chopped onions

Combine all ingredients. Mixture will be soft. Shape into walnut-sized balls. Place meatballs on baking sheet in a 400° oven. Bake until no longer pink. Combine all sauce ingredients. Place meatballs in a baking dish and pour sauce over meatballs. Bake at 350° for 1 hour.

Swedish Meatballs

1 lb. hamburger
½ c. cracker crumbs
½ c. water
1 tsp. salt
⅛ tsp. celery salt
⅛ tsp. garlic salt
⅛ tsp. pepper

Sauce:
1 onion, grated
1 can cream of mushroom soup
1 can water

Mix and make into small balls. Brown meatballs. Mix together sauce ingredients. Pour over meatballs. Bake at 350° for 1 hour.

Main Dishes

Mini Cheddar Meat Loaves

1 lb. hamburger
1 egg
½ c. oatmeal
½ c. chopped onion
1 tsp. salt
¾ c. milk
1 c. shredded cheddar cheese

Sauce:
⅔ c. ketchup
½ c. brown sugar
1½ tsp. mustard

Mix and shape into 2 loaves. Mix sauce ingredients well and spoon over loaves. Bake uncovered at 350° for 1 hour.

Mock Ham Loaf

1 lb. hamburger
½ lb. hot dogs, ground
1 c. cracker crumbs
1 egg
salt and pepper

Sauce:
6 Tbsp. brown sugar
⅓ c. tomato juice
⅜ tsp. mustard
⅓ c. water
⅞ Tbsp. vinegar

water
clear jel

Mix half of sauce with meat mixture. Cook other half a few minutes and thicken with a little clear jel and water. Pour over ham loaf when half done. Bake at 350° for 1½ hours.

Mock Ham Loaf

1 lb. hamburger
½ lb. hot dogs, ground
1 c. cracker crumbs
1 egg, beaten
1½ tsp. vinegar
1 tsp. salt
½ c. brown sugar
¼ c. water
¼ tsp. dry mustard

Mix and form into a loaf. Bake at 350° for 1¼ hours.

Savory Meat Loaf

1 lb. hamburger
½ c. oatmeal or cracker crumbs
⅛ tsp. pepper
2 Tbsp. ketchup
2 Tbsp. minced onions
1¼ tsp. salt
1 sm. egg, beaten
½ tsp. mustard

Mix and form into a loaf. Bake at 350° for 1 hour uncovered. When half done, cut into pieces and spread with glaze. Bake until done.

Glaze:
¼ c. brown sugar
1½ tsp. Worcestershire sauce
¾ tsp. mustard
2 Tbsp. ketchup

Barbecue Sauce – for Hamburgers, Ribs, etc.

1 c. ketchup, preferably homemade
1 Tbsp. Worcestershire sauce
¾ Tbsp. mustard
6 Tbsp. brown sugar
1 Tbsp. chili powder

Mix all together. If sauce is left over from barbecuing it can be kept in refrigerator for several weeks.

Steak Marinade

⅓ c. soy sauce
3 Tbsp. chopped onion
½ tsp. sesame oil
¾ c. vegetable oil
¼ tsp. garlic powder

Mix well. Marinate steak overnight.

Chicken Fried Steaks

1 lb. hamburger
½ c. flour
1 tsp. salt
¼ tsp. pepper
1 lg. egg
cracker crumbs

Mix meat, flour, salt and pepper so that it sticks together and can be rolled out in ¼" steaks cut in desired size. Dip into beaten egg, then roll into cracker crumbs. Fry in butter for about 7 minutes on each side. These can be frozen without being fried.

Barbecue Sauce – for Chicken

½ c. vinegar
½ Tbsp. Worcestershire sauce
½ c. water
¼ c. butter
1⅜ Tbsp. salt

Grilled Chicken Breasts

2 lb. boneless, skinless
  chicken breasts
Italian salad dressing

Cut chicken in thin slices (not too thin). Pour dressing over it until covered. Marinate overnight or for a few days. Grill over medium-high heat for approximately 8 minutes on each side.

Tender Chicken Nuggets

1 lb. boneless, skinless chicken
   breasts, cut into 1" cubes
½ c. seasoned bread crumbs
2 Tbsp. grated Parmesan cheese
1 egg white

Combine bread crumbs and Parmesan cheese. Beat the egg white. Dip the chicken pieces in egg white, then in bread crumbs. Place in a greased baking pan. Bake uncovered at 400° for 12-15 minutes or until chicken is no longer pink, turning once.

Oven-Baked Chicken

1 lb. chicken
1 c. crushed cornflakes
1½ tsp. seasoning salt
evaporated milk

Mix cornflake crumbs and seasoning salt. Dip chicken in evaporated milk then in cornflake mixture. Bake uncovered at 350° for 60-75 minutes.

Baked Garlic Chicken

4 boneless, skinless chicken
   breast halves
⅓ c. mayonnaise
⅓ c. grated Parmesan cheese
4 Tbsp. savory herb with
   garlic soup mix
2 Tbsp. dry bread crumbs

Combine mayonnaise, cheese and soup mix. Place chicken into a greased baking dish. Spread with mayonnaise mixture. Sprinkle with bread crumbs. Bake uncovered at 400° for 20-25 minutes or until meat thermometer reads 170°.

Oven-Baked Chicken Nuggets

2 boneless, skinless chicken
   breasts, cut into 1" cubes
½ c. Miracle Whip
6 Tbsp. milk
½ tsp. onion powder
¾ tsp. seasoning salt
1 c. crushed crackers

Blend Miracle Whip, milk, onion powder and seasoning salt until smooth. Dip chicken pieces into mixture then roll in crackers. Place on greased baking pan and bake at 425° for 18-20 minutes. Serve with barbecue sauce.

Pan-Fried Runion Chicken

chicken
1 c. milk
1 egg, beaten
Runion mix

Mix milk and beaten egg. Dip chicken in the batter and roll in Runion mix. Deep-fry. Put chicken in pan in single layer without water. Bake uncovered at 350° for 1 hour.

Ground Turkey Burgers

1 lb. ground turkey
1 egg, beaten
½ c. cracker crumbs
¼ tsp. seasoning salt
dash of salt and pepper

Mix all together and form into patties. In a saucepan fry in butter until no longer pink.

Mexican Chicken Roll-Ups

1½ c. cubed, fried chicken
¾ c. sour cream, divided
1½ tsp. taco seasoning, divided
½ c. cream of mushroom soup, divided
¾ c. shredded cheddar cheese, divided
¼ c. salsa
4 (7") flour tortillas
shredded lettuce
chopped tomatoes
additional salsa

In a bowl combine chicken, ¼ c. sour cream, ¾ tsp. taco seasoning, ¼ c. mushroom soup, ½ c. cheddar cheese and salsa. Divide filling between 4 tortillas. Roll up and place in greased 8" square baking dish. Combine remaining sour cream, taco seasoning and soup. Pour over tortillas. Cover and bake at 350° for 25-30 minutes or until heated through. Top with remaining cheese. Serve with lettuce, tomatoes and additional salsa if desired.

Chicken Enchiladas

1 c. chicken, cooked and diced
¼ c. diced green peppers
¼ c. chopped onions
⅛ lb. Monterey Jack cheese, shredded
½ lb. cheddar cheese, shredded
1 can cream of chicken soup
chicken broth
⅛ tsp. cumin
¼ tsp. oregano
⅛ tsp. chili powder
¼ tsp. garlic powder
4 flour tortillas
lettuce
sour cream
salsa

Grease an 8" square baking dish. Layer half of chicken and half amount of pepper, onions and cheeses. Mix soup with small amount of chicken broth; add cumin, oregano, chili powder and garlic powder. Put a thin layer on top of chicken. Place 2 tortillas on top of this. Repeat layers, saving some soup mixture and cheese for top. Bake at 350° for 25 minutes or until heated through. Serve with lettuce, sour cream and salsa.

Chicken Crescents

3 oz. cream cheese, softened
3 Tbsp. butter, softened
2 Tbsp. milk
¼ tsp. salt
2 c. cubed, cooked chicken
⅛ tsp. pepper
1 Tbsp. chopped onions
1 tube crescent rolls
melted butter
¾ c. crushed croutons

Blend cream cheese and butter until smooth. Add milk, salt, chicken, pepper and onions. Separate dough into 4 rectangles, pressing perforations to form a solid dough. Spoon ½ c. chicken mixture on each rectangle. Pull 4 corners together; seal. Brush with melted butter. Top with crushed croutons. Bake uncovered at 350° for 20-25 minutes.

Main Dishes

Wet Burrito Casserole

½ lb. hamburger
2 Tbsp. chopped onions
2 Tbsp. green peppers
½ pkg. taco seasoning
½ can refried beans
¼ c. hot water
¼ c. salsa
½ can cream of mushroom soup
¾ c. sour cream
5 med. soft flour tortillas
shredded cheddar cheese
shredded lettuce
tomatoes
sour cream

Fry hamburger, onion and green pepper together. Add taco seasoning, refried beans, water and salsa. Combine soup and sour cream. Pour half of soup mixture into 8" square baking dish. Lay out 5 tortillas. Divide hamburger mixture on each (about 1 heaping Tbsp.). Roll up and place in pan side by side. Top with soup mixture. Bake at 350° for 20 minutes. Sprinkle cheddar cheese over top. Bake for 10 minutes more. May be served with shredded lettuce, tomatoes and sour cream.

Chicken Burritos

2 c. diced, cooked chicken
1 sm. onion, chopped
¼ tsp. garlic powder
1 can cream of chicken soup
¼ tsp. chili powder
5 flour tortillas
cheddar or mozzarella cheese

Mix all together except tortillas and cheese. In a greased 8" baking dish put a small amount of chicken mixture. Top with 2 tortillas and then half of chicken mixture, two more tortillas and the rest of chicken mixture. Top with 1 tortilla. Cover with cheese. Bake covered at 350° for 1 hour.

[HINT]

Broccoli Bake—Give a new appeal to leftover cooked broccoli. Cover with white sauce or a can of cream of mushroom soup. Sprinkle with white crackers and Parmesan cheese. Bake at 350° for 25-30 minutes.

Chicken Gumbo

5 slices bread,
   lightly toasted and cubed
2 c. cooked, diced chicken
2 Tbsp. butter
2 eggs, beaten
½ c. milk
½ tsp. salt
¼ c. salad dressing
1 can celery soup
½ c. chicken broth
5 slices Velveeta cheese

Layer bread and chicken in bottom of casserole dish, reserving some bread for top. Mix remaining ingredients except Veveeta cheese together and pour over chicken. Put Velveeta cheese and reserved bread cubes on top. Bake uncovered at 350° for 1¼ hours. Can be refrigerated overnight.

Chicken Supreme

1 c. cooked, diced chicken
1 can cream of chicken soup
1 c. milk
2 Tbsp. chopped onion
¼ tsp. salt
¼ tsp. pepper
1½ Tbsp. butter
½ c. Velveeta cheese, cubed
1 c. uncooked macaroni

Combine chicken, soup, milk, onion, salt, pepper, butter and cheese. Heat until cheese is melted. Add macaroni. Refrigerate overnight. Bake at 350° for 1½ hours.

Barbecue Chicken Pizza

barbecue sauce
½ lb. boneless, skinless
   chicken breasts, grilled and
   cut into bite-sized pieces
¾ c. pineapple tidbits, drained
1 c. shredded mozzarella cheese

Use your favorite pizza dough crust or crescent rolls and press into greased 8" x 11" baking dish. Spread crust with barbecue sauce. Top with chicken, pineapples and cheese. Bake at 350° for approximately 30 minutes or until crust is baked.

Main Dishes

Chicken Biscuit Potpie

1⅔ c. frozen mixed vegetables,
   thawed
1½ c. cooked, diced chicken
1 can cream of chicken soup
1 egg
½ c. milk
1 c. biscuit mix

Combine vegetables, chicken and soup. Pour into a 9" pie plate. Mix egg, milk and biscuit mix. Pour over vegetables. Bake at 350° for 25-30 minutes or until golden brown.

Sweet and Sour Chicken Over Rice

1¼ lb. chicken breasts,
   cut in bite-sized pieces
¼ c. flour
¼ tsp. salt
⅛ tsp. garlic salt
⅛ tsp. lemon pepper
2 Tbsp. vegetable oil

Combine flour, salt, garlic salt and lemon pepper. Roll chicken in flour mixture. Fry in vegetable oil. Combine sugar and clear jel in saucepan. Add remaining ingredients. Bring to a boil and cook until thickened. Add chicken and heat. Serve over rice.

Sauce:
½ c. white sugar
1 Tbsp. clear jel
¼ c. vinegar
¼ c. pineapple juice
½ tsp. soy sauce
2 Tbsp. ketchup

Chicken and Rice Casserole

½ pkg. onion soup mix
6 Tbsp. rice
½ can cream of mushroom soup
1 c. cooked, diced chicken
1¼ c. water
Velveeta cheese slices

Layer ingredients in order given in 8" square baking dish. Bake covered at 325° for 2-3 hours. Add more water if necessary.

Easy Chicken Casserole

2 c. cooked, diced chicken
2 c. cooked macaroni
¾ c. flour
milk
1 egg yolk
4 c. chicken broth
¾ c. Velveeta cheese
salt and pepper to taste
toasted bread crumbs

Make a thin gravy by combining flour with a little milk. Beat in egg yolk and add a little more milk. Heat chicken broth and add flour mixture; cook to thicken. Add Velveeta cheese. Add salt and pepper to taste. Add chicken and macaroni. Bake uncovered at 350° for 25 minutes. Top with toasted bread crumbs. Bake for 20 minutes longer.

Dressing Noodle Casserole

dressing
cooked noodles
chicken gravy
Velveeta cheese slices

Layer in order given. Bake at 350° until hot.

Chalupas

flour tortillas
sour cream
hamburger
ketchup
brown sugar
chopped lettuce
shredded cheddar cheese
taco sauce

Deep-fry tortillas in oil until lightly browned. Drain on paper towels. To prepare meat mixture, fry hamburger until browned. Add ketchup and brown sugar. Keep hot until ready to serve. Serve in following order: flour tortillas, sour cream, meat mixture, chopped lettuce, shredded cheddar cheese and taco sauce.

Ground Turkey Casserole

1 lb. ground turkey, browned
3 lg. cooked, diced potatoes
1 can cream of mushroom soup
¼ c. chopped onions
1 pt. canned green beans
salt to taste
seasoned salt to taste
pepper to taste
½ c. milk
Velveeta cheese slices

Mix all together except cheese. Top with cheese slices. Heat covered until hot in 350° oven.

Lasagna Casserole

1 lb. hamburger
1¼ c. tomato sauce
½ tsp. salt
¼ tsp. pepper
¼ tsp. garlic powder
3 oz. cream cheese, softened
1 c. sour cream
1 c. shredded cheddar cheese, divided
7 lasagna noodles, cooked and drained

Brown hamburger; add tomato sauce, salt, pepper and garlic powder. Simmer uncovered for 15 minutes. Beat cream cheese until smooth. Add sour cream and ½ c. cheddar cheese. Spread ½ c. meat sauce in a greased 8" square baking dish. Top with 2 or 3 noodles; spread ½ c. cream cheese mixture and ⅔ c. meat sauce over noodles. Repeat layers twice. Sprinkle with remaining cheese on top. Bake uncovered at 350° for 25-30 minutes. This casserole freezes well. To use frozen casserole, thaw in refrigerator for 18 hours. Remove from refrigerator 30 minutes before baking time. Bake uncovered at 350° for 40-50 minutes.

Mexican Pizzas

2 flour tortillas
1 c. refried beans
½ c. salsa
1 tomato, diced
½ c. diced green peppers
2 Tbsp. diced onions
½ c. ripe olives, drained and sliced
½ c. shredded cheddar cheese

Place tortillas on an ungreased baking sheet. Spread with beans, salsa, tomatoes, peppers, onions, olives and cheese. Bake at 350° for 10 minutes or until cheese is melted.

Impossible Cheeseburger Pie

1 lb. hamburger
1½ c. chopped onions
½ tsp. salt
¼ tsp. pepper
1½ c. milk
3 eggs
¾ c. Bisquick
1 c. pizza sauce
Velveeta cheese slices

Grease 10" pie plate. Brown hamburger and onions; drain. Add salt and pepper. Spread in plate. Beat milk, eggs and Bisquick until smooth. Pour over hamburger. Bake at 400° for 25 minutes. Top with pizza sauce and cheese. Bake until knife inserted in center comes out clean, 5-8 minutes.

Cheeseburger Casserole

1 lb. hamburger
2 Tbsp. chopped onions
2 Tbsp. chopped green peppers
1¼ c. pizza sauce
cheese slices
1 can refrigerated biscuits

Brown hamburger with onions and green peppers. Mix with pizza sauce. Pour into casserole dish. Top with cheese slices and biscuits. Bake at 400° for 20 minutes, until biscuits are golden brown.

Main Dishes

Pizza Casserole

1 lb. hamburger
salt and pepper to taste
onions to taste
4 oz. wide or med. noodles
½ can cream of mushroom soup
1 c. pizza sauce
⅛ tsp. garlic powder
2 Tbsp. Parmesan cheese
⅛ tsp. oregano
green peppers
mushrooms
mozzarella cheese
pepperoni

Brown hamburger; season with salt, pepper and onion to taste. Cook noodles for 3-5 minutes in water; drain. Place in bottom of casserole dish. Add hamburger mixture and remaining ingredients, except for mozzarella cheese and pepperoni. Top with mozzarella cheese and pepperoni. Bake covered at 350° for 40 minutes. Uncover and bake for 20 minutes longer.

Bubble Pizza

½ lb. hamburger
7-8 oz. pizza sauce
1 tube refrigerated biscuits
⅓ c. shredded cheddar cheese
¾ c. shredded mozzarella cheese

Brown hamburger; drain. Stir in pizza sauce. Add pepperoni, onions and green peppers, etc. Cut biscuits in small pieces and put in single layer in bottom of greased 8" square baking dish. Top with hamburger mixture. Bake uncovered at 400° for 20-25 minutes. Sprinkle with cheese and bake for 5 minutes longer or until cheese is melted.

[H I N T]

Taco Meat Turnaround—Put a layer of Tater Tots in a baking dish and bake according to package directions. Top with taco meat and mozzarella cheese. Bake until meat is hot and cheese is melted. Serve squares of this casserole with leftover taco toppings.

Upside-Down Pizza

1 lb. hamburger
1 Tbsp. chopped onion
salt and pepper to taste
1 c. pizza sauce
12 slices pepperoni
green peppers, optional
mushrooms
1 c. sour cream
½ c. mozzarella cheese
1 tube crescent rolls

Brown hamburger and onions; add salt and pepper to taste. Add pizza sauce and put into an 8" square baking dish. Layer with pepperoni, green peppers and mushrooms. Bake at 350° for 15-20 minutes. Remove from oven and cover with sour cream and mozzarella cheese. Top with crescent rolls and bake until rolls are done.

Taco Bake

1 c. flour
¼ tsp. cream of tartar
2 tsp. baking powder
¼ tsp. salt
¼ c. butter, softened
⅓ c. milk
1 lb. hamburger
½ can pork and beans
½ pkg. taco seasoning
1½ c. pizza sauce
2 Tbsp. chopped onions
¾ c. sour cream
⅓ c. Miracle Whip
cheddar cheese
salsa
lettuce

Mix together flour, cream of tartar, baking powder, salt, butter and milk and pat into a greased 8" square baking dish. Fry hamburger and add pork and beans, taco seasoning, pizza sauce and onions. Put on top of dough. Mix sour cream and Miracle Whip. Spread on hamburger mixture. Top with cheddar cheese. Bake at 350° for 30 minutes. Serve with salsa and lettuce.

Main Dishes

Vegetable Rice Medley

½ c. uncooked rice
1⅛ c. water
1½ tsp. onion or chicken soup base
⅛ tsp. salt
1 c. frozen mixed vegetables

In a saucepan, combine the rice, water, soup base and salt. Bring to a boil. Add vegetables; boil again. Reduce heat; cover and simmer for 15 minutes or until tender.

Hamburger Rice Casserole

1 lb. hamburger
½ med. onion, chopped
salt to taste
¾ c. diced celery
1 can cream of mushroom soup
¼ c. uncooked rice
1¼ c. water
pepper

Fry hamburger, onion, salt and celery in skillet until hamburger is browned. Mix together soup, rice, water and pepper and add to hamburger mixture. Put in baking dish. Bake at 250° for 2 hours. Top with Velveeta cheese slices.

Spaghetti

1 lb. hamburger, browned
  with onions
6 Tbsp. brown sugar
½ tsp. Parmesan cheese
¾ tsp. garlic powder
2½ pt. pizza sauce
½ can cream of mushroom soup
¾ tsp. salt
8 oz. spaghetti, cooked
½ tsp. black pepper

Mix all together and bake at 350° until heated thoroughly. This can be frozen.

[HINT]

For quick tasty tacos, put leftover chili in taco shells.
Add cheese, lettuce, tomatoes and sour cream.

Simple Hamburger Noodle Casserole

1 lb. hamburger
1 Tbsp. chopped onions
salt and pepper to taste
4 oz. med. noodles
1 can cream of mushroom soup
½ can milk
Velveeta cheese

Fry hamburger and onions; add salt and pepper to taste. Cook noodles; add salt. Mix soup and milk. Mix all together and put into baking dish. Top with Velveeta cheese slices. Bake at 350° for 30 minutes or until hot.

Ground Beef Spaghetti Casserole

¼ lb. spaghetti, cooked for
   10 minutes
½ lb. hamburger, browned
1 can cream of mushroom soup
½ c. milk
½ c. Miracle Whip
Velveeta cheese
salt to taste

Drain spaghetti and mix with hamburger. Melt soup, milk, Miracle Whip, cheese and salt over low heat. Mix with spaghetti and hamburger. Heat.

El Paso Casserole

6 oz. noodles
½ lb. Velveeta cheese
½ lb. chipped ham

White Sauce:
4 Tbsp. butter
4 Tbsp. flour
2 c. milk

Melt butter; add flour. Stir until smooth. Turn off heat and add milk. Boil for 1 minute. Cook noodles in water, not too soft. Blend cheese and ham into white sauce. Pour over noodles into buttered pan. Sprinkle with toasted bread crumbs. Bake uncovered at 350° for 30 minutes or until hot.

Main Dishes

Hamburger Macaroni Casserole

1 lb. hamburger, browned
1 can cream of mushroom soup
1 can cream of chicken soup
1 can water
1 c. uncooked macaroni
¼ lb. Velveeta cheese

Mix all together and bake for 1 hour at 350°.

Ground Beef Grand Style

1 lb. hamburger
¼ c. onions, chopped
6 oz. cream cheese
salt to taste
¼ c. ketchup
¼ c. milk
1 can cream of mushroom soup
1 can refrigerated biscuits

Fry hamburger and onions until browned. Add cream cheese, salt, ketchup, milk and soup. Bake at 350° for 15 minutes. Place biscuits on top and bake for 15 minutes longer.

Meat Loaf Tater Tot Casserole

½ c. tomato juice
1 sm. egg, beaten
½ tsp. salt
1 lb. hamburger
⅜ c. oatmeal
⅛ tsp. onion salt
⅛ tsp. pepper
½ can cream of mushroom soup
Tater Tots

Mix all together except soup and Tater Tots. Press into 8" square baking dish. Top with soup and Tater Tots. Bake at 350° until meat is no longer pink.

[H I N T]

Broccoli Stretcher—Nothing goes to waste if you slice leftover broccoli stems and cook them with sliced carrots.

Italian Delight

1 lb. hamburger
chopped onion
salt and pepper to taste
1 pt. corn, salted
4 oz. noodles, cooked for 5 min.
½ can cream of mushroom soup
1 can cream of chicken soup
¼ lb. Velveeta cheese, cubed
½ pkg. saltine crackers
2 Tbsp. butter, melted

Brown hamburger with onion. Mix all together except for crackers and butter. Put in casserole dish. Crush crackers. Sauté in butter. Put buttered crumbs on top. Bake uncovered at 350° for 30 minutes; uncover and bake for 45 minutes longer. Baking time varies, depending if casserole is warm or cold when put in oven.

Mock Turkey Casserole

1 lb. hamburger
chopped onions
1 can cream of mushroom soup
½ can cream of celery soup
2 c. milk
½ loaf bread, toasted
salt and pepper to taste

Brown hamburger with onions. Mix all together and put in greased casserole dish. Bake covered at 350° for 30 minutes. Uncover and bake 15-20 minutes longer.

Mock Turkey with Vegetables

1 lb. hamburger, browned
½ loaf bread, toasted and cubed
1½ c. milk
salt and pepper to taste
1 can cream of chicken soup
½ can cream of celery soup
1 pt. canned carrots and potatoes

Mix all together and put in greased casserole dish. Bake uncovered at 350° for 45-60 minutes.

Main Dishes

Poor Man's Steak

1 lb. hamburger
1 tsp. salt
1 c. milk
1 can cream of mushroom soup
1 c. cracker crumbs
¼ tsp. pepper
1 Tbsp. chopped onion

Sauce:
1½ can cream of mushroom soup
1 sm. onion, chopped
1½ Tbsp. ketchup
1 tsp. Worcestershire sauce
small amount water
small amount liquid smoke

Mix all ingredients. Shape into a loaf and refrigerate overnight. Slice and roll in flour. Fry in butter until browned; put in roaster. Make sauce and pour over meat. Bake at 350° for 1 hour.

Shipwreck Casserole

1 lb. hamburger
chopped onions
salt to taste
2 c. cubed potatoes
1 c. peas
1 c. diced carrots
1 can cream of chicken soup,
    mixed with some milk
Velveeta cheese

Brown hamburger with onions and salt. Cook vegetables separately; season with salt. Layer hamburger, vegetables and soup. Bake at 350° for 1 hour or more until hot. Put Velveeta cheese on top. Return to oven until cheese is melted.

[HINT]
Piercing chicken drumsticks or breasts with a fork, improves the flavor if you are marinating them.

Stromboli

1½ tsp. yeast
½ c. warm water
½ tsp. white sugar
2 Tbsp. olive oil
⅛ tsp. salt
1½ c. bread flour
½ lb. hamburger, browned
½ c. cubed ham
½ c. pizza sauce
salt and pepper to taste
garlic salt to taste
½ c. sour cream
Ranch dressing mix
shredded mozzarella cheese
shredded cheddar cheese
beaten egg white
celery seed

Dissolve yeast in warm water. Add sugar, oil, salt and flour. Knead until smooth. Let rise for 40 minutes. Mix together hamburger, cubed ham, pizza sauce, salt, pepper and garlic salt. Roll out dough in a 9" x 6" rectangle. Spread meat mixture down the center. Mix ½ c. sour cream with Ranch dressing mix. Spread over meat. Sprinkle with shredded mozzarella cheese and cheddar cheese. Fold dough over meat and pinch to seal. Place seam-side down on greased baking sheet. Brush with beaten egg white and sprinkle with celery seed. Bake at 350° for 30 minutes.

Crusty Pizza Casserole

¾ c. flour
⅓ tsp. salt
1 tsp. baking powder
¼ c. milk
2 Tbsp. vegetable oil
½ c. spaghetti, broken
1 lb. hamburger
2 Tbsp. chopped onion
1 pt. pizza sauce

Topping:
½ c. sour cream
1½ Tbsp. Miracle Whip
1½ c. mozzarella cheese
milk for desired consistency

Mix flour, salt and baking powder. Add milk and oil. Press into bottom of 9" x 13" pan and bake at 350° just until done. Cook spaghetti; drain. Brown hamburger and onions; drain. Add pizza sauce. Mix with spaghetti. Pour over baked crust. Combine topping ingredients and spread over top. Bake at 350° until heated through.

Pizza

Toppings:
pizza sauce
1 lb. sausage, browned
¼ c. cubed ham
2 Tbsp. chopped onions
2 Tbsp. chopped green peppers
¼ c. bacon, crumbled
12 pepperonis
¼ lb. mozzarella cheese, shredded

Use your favorite crust recipe. Bake at
375° for 30 minutes.

Cheesy Biscuit Cups

½ lb. hamburger
1 c. spaghetti sauce
1 tube refrigerated biscuits
½ c. shredded cheddar cheese

Brown hamburger; drain. Stir in
spaghetti sauce. Cook over medium
heat for 5-10 minutes or until heated
through. Press biscuits into the bottom
and up the sides of greased muffin
cups. Spoon 2 Tbsp. meat mixture into
the center. Bake at 375° for 15-17
minutes or until golden brown.
Sprinkle with cheese and bake for 3
minutes longer until cheese is melted.

[H I N T]

*When covering cheese topped dishes with foil before baking,
first coat the underside of the foil with nonstick cooking spray.
That way the melted cheese won't come off with the foil.*

Hamburger Crescent Pie

1 lb. hamburger
½ c. chopped onions
8 oz. tomato sauce
2 Tbsp. taco seasoning
1 tube crescent rolls
1½ c. crushed nacho chips,
    divided
1 c. sour cream
1 c. shredded cheddar cheese

Cook hamburger and onion until meat is browned; drain. Stir in tomato sauce and taco seasoning. Bring to a boil and simmer uncovered for 5 minutes. Separate crescent rolls into 8 triangles. Place in a greased 9" pie plate with points toward the center. Press into bottom and up the sides. Sprinkle 1 c. chips over crust. Top with meat mixture. Spread sour cream over meat. Sprinkle with cheese and remaining chips. Bake at 350° for 20-25 minutes or until cheese is melted and crust is golden brown. Let set for 5 minutes before cutting.

Skillet Meal

½ lb. hamburger
¼ c. chopped onion
½ can cream of mushroom soup
⅓ c. mushrooms, undrained
2 med. potatoes,
    cooked and sliced
1 c. green beans
4 slices Velveeta cheese

Brown hamburger and onions. Add soup and mushrooms with liquid. Stir and heat until bubbly. Add potatoes and green beans, stirring well. Heat through. Top with cheese and melt.

Doggies on Sticks

½ lb. hot dogs, cut in half
1 egg yolk
¼ c. milk
½ c. biscuit mix
⅛ tsp. paprika
¼ tsp. dry mustard
dash of pepper

Heat deep-frying oil to 375°. Combine egg yolk and milk. Stir in dry ingredients and mix well. Place toothpicks in hot dogs and dip in batter. Deep-fry until golden.

Baked Beans

3 slices bacon,
   cooked and crumbled
¼ lb. hamburger, browned
¼ c. chopped onions
1 (16 oz.) can pork and beans
1 c. lima beans
¼ c. ketchup
¼ c. white sugar
¼ c. brown sugar
1 Tbsp. mustard
½ tsp. salt
¼ c. barbecue sauce
1 Tbsp. molasses

Combine bacon, hamburger, onion and beans. Mix remaining ingredients. Combine with bean mixture. Heat in saucepan until hot.

Pineapple Sauce for Ham

2 Tbsp. water
¾ c. brown sugar
¾ Tbsp. ketchup
¾ Tbsp. soy sauce
¾ tsp. dry mustard
¾ c. crushed pineapples
   with juice
4 tsp. clear jel
¼ c. water

Combine 2 Tbsp. water, sugar, ketchup, soy sauce, mustard and pineapples in a saucepan. Bring to a boil and simmer for 10 minutes. Dissolve clear jel in ¼ c. water. Add to sauce, cooking until clear. Serve over ham slices.

Cheesy Noodle Casserole

8 oz. pkg. med. egg noodles
2 Tbsp. butter
2 Tbsp. flour
¼ tsp. garlic salt
2 Tbsp. butter
1½ c. milk
½ lb. Velveeta cheese

Topping:
¼ c. dry bread crumbs
1 Tbsp. butter, melted

Cook noodles according to package directions; drain. In a saucepan melt butter. Stir in flour and garlic and onion salts until smooth. Gradually stir in milk. Bring to a boil. Cook for 2 minutes until thickened. Add the cheese; stir until melted. Add noodles. Transfer to a greased 1 qt. baking dish. Toss bread crumbs and butter; sprinkle over casserole. Bake uncovered at 350° for 20-25 minutes.

Green Beans and Rice Skillet

2 Tbsp. olive oil or butter
1 qt. canned green beans
1 pt. canned beef chunks
prepared rice

In a large skillet put oil or butter. Drain green beans. Pour into skillet. Add beef chunks. Fry over medium heat until beans are browned. Delicious served with rice.

Fried Green Beans

2 Tbsp. olive oil or butter
1 qt. canned green beans
salt and pepper to taste

In a large skillet put oil or butter. Drain green beans. Pour beans into skillet and fry over medium heat until browned. Sprinkle with salt and pepper.

Lemon Green Beans

1 qt. canned green beans
½ tsp. lemon juice
¼ tsp. salt
⅛ tsp. pepper
1 Tbsp. butter

In a saucepan heat green beans. Add lemon juice, salt, pepper and butter. Heat until hot and serve.

Main Dishes

[H I N T]

Baked potatoes should be pricked with a fork to release the steam as soon as they are finished baking. This will keep them from getting soggy.

[H I N T]

Don't waste time scrubbing your grill rack. Put it in a plastic trash bag and spray it generously with oven cleaner. Close tightly and leave overnight. Cleaning the rack the next day will be a breeze.

Soups, Salads and Sandwiches

Eating can be such an adventure! Especially in a foreign country where you not only don't speak the language (you just hope the waiter brings what you think you ordered), but their way of eating isn't exactly second nature to you.

One of my unforgettable eating experiences was while on a mission trip to China back in 1998. While in Beijing, a small group of us decided to do some sight-seeing around the city. Sarah, our Chinese guide, took us to a local restaurant that specialized in noodles.

First we watched the chef take a hunk of dough and form it into a circle. Then he deftly pulled, twisted and folded it until he had strings of noodles dangling from his hands. Next he tossed them into a kettle of boiling water. Obviously, it wasn't his first day.

Now for the challenge: How do you eat long, slippery noodles with only a pair of chopsticks at your disposal? Step 1. After numerous attempts, you finally manage to capture one end of a noodle between the wooden sticks protruding from between your fingers. Step 2. Slowly you lift the noodle in the general direction of your mouth. Noodle slips back into bowl. Step 3. Same as Step 1. Step 4. Now you've maneuvered one end of the pasta into your mouth. (Make sure Mom isn't looking.) Apply suction; the rest will follow. That's all there's to it. By the look on the faces of the other restaurant patrons, we did provide some amusement for them!

—*Sam*

Chili Soup

¾ lb. hamburger
½ tsp. salt
¼ tsp. chili powder
½ tsp. Worcestershire sauce
1 qt. tomato juice
½ c. ketchup
½ c. brown sugar
1 c. kidney beans

Brown hamburger and drain. Add salt, chili powder and Worcestershire sauce. Simmer for a few minutes. Add tomato juice, ketchup and sugar. Simmer for 5 minutes. Add beans and simmer for 15 minutes or longer. Thicken with clear jel for a thicker soup.

Taco Soup

½ lb. hamburger
1 Tbsp. chopped onion
¼ c. flour
2 c. tomato juice
½ c. brown sugar
1 c. pork and beans
1 Tbsp. taco seasoning
taco chips
shredded cheddar cheese
sour cream

Brown hamburger and onion. Add flour to hamburger. Add tomato juice, sugar, beans and seasoning. Simmer for 1 hour. Serve over crushed taco chips. Sprinkle cheese on top and add sour cream.

Chicken Chowder Soup

1 c. chicken broth
½ c. diced celery
½ c. diced potatoes
½ c. diced carrots
1 Tbsp. butter
¼ tsp. salt
⅓ c. flour
1 c. milk
½ c. Velveeta cheese
1 c. deboned, diced chicken

Mix broth, vegetables, butter and salt; bring to a boil. Slowly add flour mixed with milk. Bring to a boil. Add cheese and chicken.

Soups, Salads and Sandwiches

Hearty Ham Soup

½ c. diced carrots
½ c. diced potatoes
⅓ c. diced onions
⅓ c. diced celery
½ tsp. chicken base
2 c. milk
¾ c. cubed ham
clear jel

Cover vegetables with water; add chicken base. Cook until tender. Add milk and ham. Thicken with clear jel mixed with a little water. Add Velveeta cheese and salt to taste.

Comforting Chicken Noodle Soup

½ qt. water
2 chicken bouillon cubes
1½ c. uncooked med. noodles
½ can cream of chicken soup
¾ c. diced, cooked chicken
¼ c. sour cream

Bring water and bouillon cubes to a boil. Add noodles; cook uncovered until tender for approximately 10 minutes. Do not drain. Add soup and chicken; heat through. Remove from heat; stir in sour cream. Serve immediately.

Country Potato Soup

1½ c. potatoes, diced
¼ c. diced carrots
¼ c. chopped onion
¾ c. water
1 chicken bouillon cube
¼ tsp. salt
1 c. milk
½ c. sour cream
1 Tbsp. flour
½ tsp. chopped chives, optional

Combine potatoes, carrots, onions, water, bouillon cube and salt in a saucepan. Cover and cook until vegetables are tender but not mushy. Add ½ c. milk; heat. Mix sour cream, flour, chives and remaining milk. Stir mixture into soup base gradually. Cook over low heat, stirring constantly, until thickened. Add Velveeta cheese for extra flavor.

Cream of Mushroom Soup

1½ Tbsp. butter
1 Tbsp. flour
½ tsp. salt
dash of pepper
1 c. half and half
1 c. chicken broth
¼ tsp. onion salt
½ c. chopped mushrooms,
   sautéed

Melt butter; add flour, salt and pepper. Remove from heat and stir in half and half and chicken broth. Boil for 1 minute. Add onion salt and mushrooms. Cook until heated through. Serve.

Noodle Broccoli Cheese Soup

½ Tbsp. chopped onion
1½ c. chicken broth
2 oz. fine noodles
½ pkg. frozen chopped broccoli
1½ c. milk
1 c. Velveeta cheese
salt and pepper to taste

In a saucepan melt butter; add onions and sauté over medium heat for 3 minutes. Add chicken broth; heat to boiling. Gradually add noodles and salt so that the broth continues to boil. Cook uncovered for 3 minutes, stirring occasionally. Stir in broccoli. Cook 4 minutes longer. Add milk, cheese, salt and pepper. Continue cooking until cheese melts, stirring occasionally.

[H I N T]

To use up leftover mixed vegetables, combine one cup of vegetables with a can of cream of chicken soup. Add milk and heat through for a delicious thick soup.

Soups, Salads and Sandwiches

Broccoli Soup

1 c. chicken broth
1 chicken bouillon cube
1½ c. chopped broccoli
1 Tbsp. chopped onion
1½ Tbsp. butter
2 Tbsp. flour
¼ tsp. salt
dash of pepper
1¼ c. milk
½ c. Velveeta cheese
½ c. mashed potatoes

Simmer broth, bouillon cube and broccoli until tender. Simmer onion, butter, flour, salt and pepper in saucepan. Stir until thick. Add milk and Velveeta cheese. Stir in broccoli mixture, then add the mashed potatoes last. Stir over low heat until heated through.

Cheesy Turkey Chowder

1-1½ c. turkey meat or
  ground turkey with broth
chicken flavored seasoning
½ c. chopped celery
2 Tbsp. chopped onion
½ c. chopped carrots
½ c. diced potatoes
3 Tbsp. flour
1 c. milk
2 Tbsp. butter
½ c. shredded cheese or
  4 oz. Velveeta cheese
salt, optional

Heat meat and broth; add water to make 2 c. broth. Add chicken flavored seasoning to taste. Add vegetables; simmer until tender. Blend flour and milk until smooth. Stir into broth along with butter and cheese. Stir constantly until thickened. Add salt if necessary.

[HINT]

Chili Saver—Freeze leftover chili in muffin cups. Later you can have an easy chili dog by heating a portion and serving it over a cooked hot dog.

Hearty Hamburger Soup

½ lb. hamburger
¼ c. flour
½ c. cubed carrots
½ c. cubed potatoes
1 Tbsp. butter
2 c. milk
1 c. tomato juice
½ tsp. seasoned salt
¾ tsp. salt

Fry hamburger; add flour. Cook carrots and potatoes. Melt butter; add milk, tomato juice and seasonings. Add hamburger, carrots and potatoes. Heat thoroughly; do not boil.

Cracker Soup

¾ qt. milk
1 Tbsp. butter
saltine crackers

In a small saucepan, heat milk and butter until scalding. Pour into soup bowls and add crumbled saltine crackers. Delicious served with tuna salad.

Amish Church Baby Soup

1 Tbsp. butter
¾ qt. milk
cubed bread
salt and pepper to taste

In a small saucepan, brown butter. Add milk. When milk is warm, add enough cubed bread until right consistency. Add salt and pepper to taste. Heat a few minutes longer.

Rivel Soup

1 c. flour
½ tsp. salt
1 egg
1 qt. scalding milk

Mix salt with flour; toss egg lightly through flour mixture until small crumbs form. Stir into scalding milk. Bring to a boil and serve at once.

Soups, Salads and Sandwiches

Oriental Salad

chopped lettuce
shredded cheese
Ramen noodles,
   toasted in butter
sweet and sour dressing, or
   dressing of your choice

Mix lettuce, cheese and noodles just before serving. Serve with dressing.

Cauliflower and Broccoli Salad

¼ head cauliflower
½ head broccoli
4 oz. shredded cheddar cheese
½ lb. bacon, fried and crumbled
½ c. Miracle Whip
¼ pkg. Ranch dressing mix
2 Tbsp. white sugar
1 tsp. vinegar

Chop vegetables. Toss vegetables, cheese and bacon. Combine Miracle Whip, dressing mix, sugar and vinegar. Pour over salad. Mix lightly and chill.

[HINT]

Here's a way to use those leftover waffles or pancakes. Spread one side with peanut butter and jelly. Top with a second pancake. Butter the outsides and grill as you would a grilled cheese sandwich.

Pasta Salad

½ lb. spiral macaroni,
   cooked, drained and cooled
2 Tbsp. chopped green pepper
¼ c. ripe olives, optional
2 Tbsp. minced onion
2 oz. diced ham
2 Tbsp. chopped celery
tomatoes, optional

Dressing:
½ c. Miracle Whip
¼ c. mayonnaise
1 Tbsp. Dijonaise creamy blend mustard
1 Tbsp. salad oil
2 Tbsp. vinegar
½ c. white sugar
1 tsp. onion salt
1 tsp. celery seed

Mix ingredients together. Combine dressing ingredients. Mix well and pour over pasta.

Simple Taco Salad

1 c. flour
1 tsp. white sugar
¼ tsp. salt
¼ c. shortening
2 tsp. baking powder
¼ tsp. cream of tartar
⅓ c. milk
½ c. sour cream
3 oz. cream cheese
½ lb. hamburger
1 Tbsp. taco seasoning
½ c. pizza sauce
grated cheese
lettuce
tomatoes
crushed taco chips
hot sauce

Combine flour, sugar, salt, shortening, baking powder, cream of tartar and milk. Spread into greased 8" square baking dish. Bake at 350° for 12-15 minutes or until toothpick inserted in center comes out clean. Cool. Mix sour cream and softened cream cheese. Spread on cooled crust. Brown hamburger; stir in taco seasoning and pizza sauce. When cooled spread on top of sour cream layer. Top with shredded cheese. Serve with lettuce, tomatoes, taco chips and hot sauce.

Taco Salad

¼ head lettuce, shredded
¼ lb. hamburger, browned
   and cooled
1 Tbsp. taco seasoning
3 oz. cheddar cheese
¼ can kidney beans
1 c. crushed taco chips

Dressing:
¾ c. Thousand Island dressing
2 Tbsp. white sugar
1 tsp. taco seasoning
1 tsp. taco sauce

Mix hamburger with taco seasoning. Toss with lettuce. Add cheese, beans and taco chips. Mix with dressing.

10-Minute Taco Salad

2 c. crushed corn chips
1 c. chili beans, undrained
½ c. shredded cheddar cheese
1 c. chopped lettuce
½ c. salsa
¼ c. sour cream

Place corn chips on a flat serving dish. Heat beans until hot; pour over chips. Top with cheese, lettuce, salsa and sour cream. For an attractive look, drop sour cream by tsp. over the top. Serve immediately.

Potato Salad (1)

4 c. cooked, shredded
   potatoes, cooled
3 hard-boiled eggs, cut up
1½ Tbsp. chopped celery

Dressing:
1 c. Miracle Whip
1 Tbsp. vinegar
½ tsp. salt
1½ Tbsp. mustard
½ c. white sugar

Mix dressing ingredients and pour over potato mixture. Mix well and chill.

[H I N T]

When frying bacon, sprinkle a little sugar in the skillet. The bacon won't stick to the pan.

Soups, Salads and Sandwiches

Potato Salad (2)

3 c. shredded potatoes,
    cooked and cooled
1 Tbsp. chopped onion
3 hard-boiled eggs,
    cooled and shredded
½ c. chopped celery

Dressing:
¾ c. Miracle Whip
1 Tbsp. vinegar
¼ tsp. salt
¾ Tbsp. mustard
½ c. white sugar
2 Tbsp. milk

Mix dressing ingredients well and add to potato mixture. Refrigerate. Salad is best if chilled for at least 12 hours.

Layered Coleslaw

shredded cabbage
dressing
fried and crumbled bacon
shredded cheddar cheese
salad topping

Dressing:
¼ c. salad dressing
⅛ tsp. celery seed
2 Tbsp. vegetable oil
¼ c. + 2 Tbsp. white sugar
2 Tbsp. milk
1 Tbsp. mustard
2 Tbsp. vinegar
¼ tsp. onion salt
2 oz. cream cheese

Mix dressing ingredients well. Layer on plate in order given.

Dressing for Coleslaw

1 c. salad dressing
¼ tsp. salt
1½ tsp. mustard
½ c. white sugar
5 Tbsp. milk

Mix well and serve with shredded cabbage.

Coleslaw (1)

¼ head cabbage, shredded
¼ c. chopped green peppers, optional
¼ c. chopped celery
¼ c. shredded carrots
½ tsp. salt
½ c. white sugar
¼ tsp. celery seed
⅛ tsp. mustard seed
2 Tbsp. vinegar

Mix together salt, sugar, celery seed, mustard seed and vinegar and add to rest of ingredients. Chill. This can also be frozen.

Coleslaw (2)

¼ head cabbage, shredded
chopped green peppers, optional
shredded carrots, optional

Dressing:
¼ c. white sugar
2 Tbsp. vinegar
2 Tbsp. vegetable oil

Mix dressing ingredients well and toss with cabbage.

Lettuce and Chicken Salad

¼ head lettuce, shredded
¼ head broccoli, chopped
¼ c. sliced radishes
2 Tbsp. chopped celery
¼ c. French-fried onions
¼ c. shredded carrots
½ c. shredded cheddar cheese
1 c. cut-up chicken, fried tender

Dressing:
¼ c. mayonnaise
¼ c. sour cream
2 Tbsp. sweet cream
2 Tbsp. white sugar
1½ Tbsp. red wine vinegar

Mix dressing ingredients well. Toss with lettuce and chicken mixture just before serving.

Vegetable Pizza

8 oz. crescent rolls
3 oz. cream cheese
½ c. sour cream
1 Tbsp. Ranch dressing mix
broccoli
cauliflower
carrots
cheddar cheese
bacon bits

Grease an 8" square pan and press in crescent rolls. Not all of the rolls may be needed. Bake at 350° for 12-15 minutes or until done. Cool. Mix cream cheese, sour cream and dressing mix. Spread onto crust. Top with chopped vegetables, cheese and bacon or whatever you wish. Chill.

[H I N T]

*Scalloped Potato Soup—Leftover scalloped potatoes
can easily be stretched to make soup. Combine potatoes
with mixed vegetables, cream of mushroom, chicken
or celery soup and some milk. Heat through.*

French Dressing

1 c. Miracle Whip
1 c. white sugar
2 Tbsp. vinegar
¼ c. ketchup
1 tsp. mustard
½ tsp. paprika
¼ tsp. salt
2 tsp. water
¼ c. oil
½ Tbsp. grated onion

Mix all ingredients together and refrigerate.

Mexican Salad Dressing

1 Tbsp. grated onion
½ c. white sugar
½ tsp. salt
¼ tsp. pepper
½ tsp. celery seed
1½ tsp. mustard
2 Tbsp. vinegar
½ c. vegetable oil
1 Tbsp. Miracle Whip

Blend all ingredients in blender until well mixed. Refrigerate.

Sweet and Sour Dressing

1 c. Miracle Whip
¼ c. white sugar
¼ c. vegetable oil
1 Tbsp. vinegar
1½ tsp. mustard
¼ tsp. celery seed

Mix until blended. Refrigerate.

Soups, Salads and Sandwiches

Thousand Island Dressing

1 c. Miracle Whip
2 Tbsp. white sugar
¼ tsp. salt
½ c. ketchup
¼ c. pickle relish

Mix well until blended. Refrigerate.

Orange Pineapple Jell-O Salad

¼ c. + 2 Tbsp. orange Jell-O
2 Tbsp. pineapple Jell-O
3 Tbsp. white sugar
1½ c. boiling water
1½ c. cold water
mandarin oranges
pineapples, crushed or chunks

Stir Jell-O and sugar in boiling water until dissolved. Add cold water. Refrigerate until slightly chilled, then add mandarin oranges and pineapples. Chill.

Apple Jell-O Salad

¼ c. + 2 Tbsp. strawberry Jell-O
2 Tbsp. orange Jell-O
3 Tbsp. white sugar
1½ c. boiling water
1½ c. cold water
shredded apples

Stir Jell-O and sugar in boiling water until dissolved. Add cold water. Refrigerate until slightly chilled, then add shredded apples. Stir and chill.

Fruit Salad

½ c. mandarin oranges
½ c. pineapple chunks
½ c. sour cream
½ c. mini marshmallows
½ c. coconut

Drain juice from oranges and pineapple. Mix together fruit, sour cream, marshmallows and coconut. Chill.

Grape Salad

3 oz. cream cheese
½ c. sour cream
¼ c. white sugar
2 Tbsp. brown sugar
1 lb. red seedless grapes
pastel mini marshmallows

Mix cream cheese and sour cream until smooth. Add sugars; mix well. Wash and drain grapes thoroughly. Mix with sauce ingredients. Gently mix in marshmallows. Refrigerate until serving.

Apple Salad

½ c. white sugar
1½ tsp. clear jel
⅛ tsp. salt
½ c. water
½ tsp. vinegar
½ tsp. vanilla
½ c. Cool Whip
4 apples
½ c. peanuts

Mix sugar, clear jel and salt in saucepan. Add water, vinegar and vanilla. Cook until clear and slightly thickened. Cool completely, then add Cool Whip. Peel and dice apples; add peanuts and sauce. Refrigerate.

Toasted Cheese Supreme

4 slices white bread
1 Tbsp. mayonnaise
3 oz. fully cooked, thin sliced ham
2 slices cheddar cheese
2 Tbsp. butter, softened

Spread 2 slices of bread with mayonnaise. Layer each with ham and cheese. Top with remaining bread. Spread butter on the outside of each sandwich. Toast sandwiches until lightly browned and cheese is melted.

[H I N T]

When you're frying bacon, line a baking pan with foil. Place bacon on top and bake in the oven at 400° until crisp.

Soups, Salads and Sandwiches

Pizza Burgers

½ lb. hamburger, browned
¼ lb. bologna
⅛ lb. pepperoni
¾ c. pizza sauce
¼ tsp. salt
dash of pepper
5 oz. Velveeta cheese
mozzarella cheese

Grind bologna and pepperoni. Mix with hamburger. Add pizza sauce, salt, pepper and Velveeta cheese. Heat until cheese melts and mixture is hot. Put on half of a bun, open face. Top with shredded mozzarella cheese. Heat in 375° oven until cheese melts. Serve immediately.

Barbecue Hamburgers

Barbecue Sauce:
¾ c. ketchup
⅓ c. brown sugar
¼ c. white sugar
2 Tbsp. honey
2 Tbsp. molasses
⅛ tsp. liquid smoke
1½ tsp. mustard
1 tsp. Worcestershire sauce
⅛ tsp. salt
dash of pepper

Burgers:
¼ c. quick oats
1 egg yolk
⅛ tsp. garlic salt
⅛ tsp. onion salt
⅛ tsp. pepper
dash of salt
1 lb. hamburger

Mix sauce ingredients; bring to a boil. Remove from heat and set aside ¾ c. to serve with burgers. Mix quick oats with egg yolk; add remaining ingredients. Mix well, then add ⅛ c. barbecue sauce. Shape into patties. Grill covered over medium heat for 6-8 minutes on each side. Baste with the barbecue sauce the last 5 minutes of grilling. Serve with remaining barbecue sauce, lettuce, tomato, mayonnaise, cheese, pickles or whatever you like.

Sloppy Joe

1 lb. hamburger
¼ c. quick oats
chopped onion, optional
1 tsp. salt
⅛ tsp. pepper
2-3 Tbsp. flour
¾ c. water
¾ c. ketchup
½ tsp. Worcestershire sauce
1½ Tbsp. mustard
¼ c. brown sugar

Mix hamburger, quick oats, onion, salt and pepper; brown. Sprinkle with flour and stir. Add water; simmer. Add ketchup, Worcestershire sauce, mustard and brown sugar. Simmer until heated through. Serve on bread or buns. Delicious with cheese and pickles.

Barbecue Ham Sandwiches

½ lb. chipped ham
1 Tbsp. flour
¾ Tbsp. brown sugar
¼ c. ketchup
1 Tbsp. vinegar
¼ c. water
¾ tsp. Worcestershire sauce

Fry meat in a little butter. Add flour and the rest of ingredients. Simmer approximately 20 minutes. Serve on bread or buns.

Ham and Cheese Sandwiches

4 slices chipped ham
2 slices Velveeta cheese
2 sandwich buns

Fix sandwich buns using 2 slices of ham and 1 slice of cheese per bun. Wrap in aluminum foil. Bake at 350° until sandwich is heated.

[H I N T]

Soup or vegetables too salty? Add a teaspoon
of sugar to remedy the situation.

Soups, Salads and Sandwiches

Table for Two

Bacon Lettuce Tomato Sandwich

4 slices bread, toasted
mayonnaise
tomatoes, sliced
½ lb. bacon, fried
lettuce

Fix sandwiches and enjoy!

Our Favorite Summertime Sandwich

4 slices bread, toasted
4 slices Swiss cheese
mayonnaise
tomatoes, sliced
salt and pepper, optional

Place cheese slices onto toasted bread.
Place on baking sheet and place in a
250° oven until cheese is melted.
Remove and spread with mayonnaise.
Top with a tomato slice. Sprinkle with
salt and pepper if desired. Enjoy!

Tuna Sandwich

1 can tuna
2 Tbsp. pickle relish
3 Tbsp. mayonnaise

Mix all together and spread on bread or
bun.

[H I N T]

*If you're in a hurry to fix a cold pasta salad, add
several ice cubes to the noodles after draining them. Stir
gently until the ice is melted and noodles are cold.*

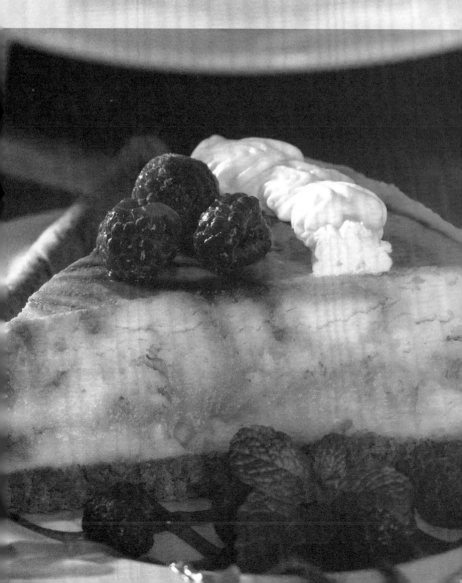

Pies

I have heard my dad and his sisters recount this story of how the neighbor boys tried to clean up the dishes for Grandma. It was oat threshing time, and as usual Grandma made a huge noon meal to feed all the hardworking men and boys who were helping. Well, mischievous boys as they were, they put their heads together and made plans to embarrass Grandma by completely cleaning up one of her menu items. What they didn't know was that Grandpa had gotten wind of this, and being warned, Grandma was well prepared.

First they tried it on the mashed potatoes, but they had to give that up for a lost cause due to the vast quantities of it. Next they attacked the pudding. The first bowlful barely made it down one side of the table before it was scraped clean. The boys' glee soon turned to dismay when Grandma just stepped into the pantry and brought out another large bowlful. After lunch was over, nearly bursting at the seams, they rolled around on the ground, groaning in misery. It's not hard to guess who had the last laugh!
                                                                    —*Sam*

Custard Pie

½ c. white sugar
½ c. brown sugar
¼ c. flour
pinch of salt
¾ tsp. vanilla
2 eggs, separated
2 c. milk

Mix sugars, flour, salt and vanilla together. Beat egg yolks and add sugar mixture; mix well. Add some milk and beat. Then add rest of milk. Beat egg whites until stiff. Fold in egg whites with rest of ingredients. Pour into unbaked pie crust. Bake in middle of oven at 450° for 10 minutes. Reduce heat to 350° and bake for 35 minutes. Reduce heat to 325° and bake for 10 minutes or until set.

Custard Pie

¾ c. white sugar
1 c. brown sugar
3 Tbsp. flour
¼ tsp. salt
1 tsp. vanilla
3 eggs, separated
2 c. milk

Mix sugars, flour, salt and vanilla together. Beat egg yolks and add to sugar mixture; mix well. Add some milk and beat. Add rest of milk. Fold in 2 beaten egg whites. Pour into 9" unbaked pie shell. Bake at 425° for 10 minutes. Reduce heat to 350° and bake for 30 minutes or until set.

Pumpkin Pie

¼ c. + 2 Tbsp. white sugar
¼ c. + 2 Tbsp. brown sugar
¾ c. pumpkin
¼ tsp. cinnamon
¼ tsp. allspice
1 Tbsp. flour
3 eggs, separated
1½ c. milk

Beat together sugars, pumpkin, cinnamon, allspice and flour. Separate eggs; beat egg yolks. Add milk. Mix together and add to sugar mixture. Beat egg whites until stiff; slowly add to rest of ingredients. Pour into unbaked pie shell. Bake at 450° for 10 minutes. Reduce heat to 350° and bake for 35 minutes. Reduce heat to 325° and bake for 10 minutes or until set.

Paradise Pumpkin Pie

8 oz. cream cheese, softened
¼ c. white sugar
½ tsp. vanilla
1 egg
1 can evaporated milk
½ c. brown sugar
2 eggs, beaten
1¼ c. pumpkin
1 tsp. cinnamon
½ tsp. pumpkin pie spice
dash of salt

Combine cream cheese, sugar and vanilla, mixing until well blended. Add egg; mix well. Spread evenly in bottom of unbaked 9" pastry crust. Combine rest of ingredients; mix well. Carefully pour over cream cheese layer. Bake at 350° for 60-65 minutes.

Pecan Pie

2 eggs
½ c. white sugar
2 Tbsp. flour
¼ tsp. salt
2 Tbsp. butter, melted
1 c. light Karo
½ c. cold water
1 c. pecans

Beat eggs, sugar, flour and salt well. Add butter, Karo, water and pecans. Bake at 450° for 12 minutes. Reduce heat to 350° and bake for approximately 30 minutes or until set.

Praline Pecan Pie

¼ c. butter
¼ c. brown sugar
⅓ c. chopped pecans
vanilla pie filling
Cool Whip

Combine butter, brown sugar and nuts in a saucepan. Heat and stir until bubbly. Spread in bottom of baked 8" pie shell and cool. Fill with your favorite vanilla pie filling. Can add some Cool Whip to filling. Top with Cool Whip.

Cream Cheese Pecan Pie

8 oz. cream cheese, softened
1 egg, beaten
1 tsp. vanilla
½ c. white sugar
½ tsp. salt
1 c. chopped pecans

Topping:
3 eggs
½ tsp. vanilla
1 c. light Karo

Cream together cream cheese, egg, vanilla, sugar and salt. Spread on bottom of unbaked 9" pie shell. Sprinkle pecans over cream cheese layer. Combine topping ingredients and beat until smooth. Pour over pecans. Bake at 375° for 35-45 minutes, until pecan layer is golden brown.

Rhubarb Pie

3 c. rhubarb, diced
2 Tbsp. flour
1½ c. white sugar
2 eggs

Crumbs:
½ c. flour
½ c. oatmeal
½ c. brown sugar
¼ c. butter

Mix rhubarb with flour and sugar; beat eggs and add to mixture. Spread into 9" unbaked pie shell. For crumbs, mix flour, oatmeal, brown sugar and butter until crumbly. Sprinkle on top of rhubarb. Bake at 425° for 10 minutes. Reduce heat to 300° and bake for 30 minutes.

Rhubarb Delight Pie

1½ c. diced rhubarb
4 Tbsp. water
¾ c. sugar
3 oz. strawberry Jell-O
1 c. Cool Whip

Cook rhubarb, water and sugar until rhubarb is soft, but not mushy. Add Jell-O; cool. When partially set, add Cool Whip and pour into 8" baked pie shell. Top with more Cool Whip if desired.

Pies

Cream Cheese Rhubarb Pie

¼ c. clear jel
1 c. sugar
½ c. water
3 c. diced rhubarb
dash of salt

Topping:
8 oz. cream cheese, softened
2 eggs
½ c. sugar

whipped topping
slivered almonds

Combine clear jel, sugar and water in a saucepan. Stir until thoroughly combined. Add rhubarb and salt. Cook, stirring often, until mixture thickens. Pour into 9" unbaked pie shell. Bake at 425° for 10 minutes. For topping, beat cream cheese, eggs and sugar until smooth. Pour over rhubarb layer. Return to oven and reduce heat to 325°. Bake until set, about 25 minutes. Cool; chill for several hours or overnight. Garnish with whipped topping and slivered almonds.

Peach Custard Pie

2 or 3 fresh peaches
¼ c. sugar
2 Tbsp. flour
¼ tsp. salt
½ c. sugar
2 eggs, separated
1½ c. milk, scalded
¼ c. sugar

Peel and slice peaches into an 8" unbaked pie shell. Sprinkle with ¼ c. sugar. Mix flour, salt and ½ c. sugar; add to beaten egg yolks. Slowly add hot milk and mix. Pour over peaches and bake at 350° until set. Beat egg whites until soft peaks form; add ¼ c. sugar. Pile on pie and bake until nicely browned.

[**H I N T**]

Pie Crust Cookies—Cut away scraps of leftover pie dough. Reroll and cut into desired shapes. Sprinkle with cinnamon and sugar. Bake at 475° for 8-10 minutes. Serve warm.

Colorado Peach Pie

4 c. fresh peaches, sliced
¼ c. white sugar
¾ c. white sugar
2 Tbsp. flour
¼ tsp. salt
1 egg
½ tsp. vanilla
1 c. sour cream

Sprinkle ¼ c. sugar over peaches; set aside. Combine ¾ c. sugar, flour, salt, egg, vanilla and sour cream. Pour into 9" unbaked pie shell. Bake at 400° for 15 minutes. Reduce heat to 350° and bake for 20 minutes. Sprinkle with crumbs. Bake at 400° for 10 more minutes.

Crumbs:
⅓ c. flour
¼ c. butter
¼ c. sugar
1 tsp. cinnamon

Raisin Pie

1 c. raisins
1 c. water
¼ tsp. baking soda
2 c. water
4 Tbsp. clear jel, mixed with water
pinch of salt
1 Tbsp. butter
1 c. brown sugar

Cook raisins, water and soda together until syrupy. Add rest of ingredients. Cook and put into unbaked pie shell with top crust. Bake at 350° for 30 minutes or until done.

Dutch Apple Pie

7 apples, peeled and shredded
½ c. brown sugar
3 Tbsp. flour
1 tsp. cinnamon
2 Tbsp. butter

Mix sugar, flour and cinnamon with apples. Put in 8" unbaked pie shell and dab with butter. Mix together crumb ingredients and put on top of apples. Bake at 375° for 45 minutes.

Crumbs:
4 Tbsp. butter, melted
¾ c. flour
½ c. brown sugar

Crumb Pie

1 c. brown sugar
½ c. light Karo
1½ c. water
1 tsp. vanilla
1 lg. egg, well beaten
½ c. flour
pinch of salt

Cook well and cool. Mix together crumb ingredients. Pour filling into a 9" unbaked pie shell. Top with crumbs. Bake at 450° for 10 minutes. Reduce heat to 350° and bake for 35 minutes. Reduce heat to 325° and bake for 10 minutes or until set.

Crumbs:
¾ c. flour
¼ c. white sugar
⅜ tsp. baking soda
⅓ tsp. cream of tartar
¼ c. shortening

[H I N T]

Tart Shells—Cut out rounds of leftover pie dough. Turn a muffin pan upside down. Press dough onto bottoms of muffin cups. Bake at 450° for 7-8 minutes until light brown. Invert pan onto wire rack. Use shells for puddings and desserts.

Southern Chess Pie

1 c. brown sugar
½ c. white sugar
2 Tbsp. flour
3 eggs, beaten
2 Tbsp. milk
½ c. butter, melted
1 tsp. vanilla
1 c. walnuts, chopped

Mix together sugars and flour. Add eggs, milk, butter, vanilla and walnuts. Pour into an unbaked pie crust. Bake at 450° for 10 minutes. Reduce heat to 350° and bake for 25 minutes.

Cream Cheese Vanilla Crumb Pie

4 oz. cream cheese, softened
¼ c. white sugar
1 egg yolk, beaten
¼ tsp. salt
½ tsp. vanilla

Filling:
1 c. water
½ c. white sugar
2 tsp. flour
½ c. dark corn syrup
1 egg yolk, beaten
½ tsp. vanilla

Crumbs:
1 c. flour
¼ c. brown sugar
¼ c. butter, softened
½ tsp. baking soda
¼ tsp. cream of tartar
¼ tsp. cinnamon

Beat together cream cheese, sugar, egg yolk, salt and vanilla until smooth. Spread in the bottom of unbaked 9" pie crust. For filling, in a saucepan bring water to a boil. Combine sugar, flour, corn syrup and egg yolk. Stir into hot water. Bring to a boil, then set aside to cool. Add vanilla. When cooled, pour over cream cheese layer. Mix the crumb ingredients until crumbly. Spread over top of pie. Bake at 375° for 30-40 minutes.

Pies

Lemon Pie

1 can sweetened condensed milk
½ c. lemon juice
8 oz. whipped topping
yellow food coloring

Combine milk and juice; let set a few minutes. Stir in whipped topping and a few drops of yellow food coloring. Pour into graham cracker crust. Chill until firm.

Lemon Cream Pie

1¼ c. water
1 c. white sugar
1 Tbsp. butter
¼ c. clear jel
6 Tbsp. lemon juice
3 egg yolks
2 Tbsp. milk

Meringue:
3 egg whites
¼ tsp. cream of tartar
6 Tbsp. white sugar
½ tsp. vanilla

Combine water, sugar and butter. Heat until sugar is dissolved. Add clear jel mixed with a little water. Cook until clear; add lemon juice and cook for 2 minutes. Add egg yolks beaten with the milk. Bring to a boil. Cool completely. Pour into an 8" baked pie crust. Top with Cool Whip or meringue. Meringue: Beat egg whites and cream of tartar until foamy. Beat in sugar, 1 Tbsp. at a time. Beat until stiff and glossy. Add vanilla. Heap onto pie filling, carefully sealing edges. Bake at 400° for 10 minutes or until golden or delicate brown.

[HINT]

For an impressive decorative top pie crust, use a thimble to cut holes in your top crust. Then replace the cutouts and bake in their holes. The holes will get bigger as the pie bakes, giving you an interesting pattern.

Sour Cream Lemon Pie

1 c. white sugar
¼ c. clear jel
⅛ tsp. salt
1 c. milk
3 egg yolks, beaten
¼ c. butter
¼ c. lemon juice
1 c. sour cream

Meringue:
3 egg whites
½ tsp. vanilla
¼ tsp. cream of tartar
6 Tbsp. sugar

In a saucepan, combine sugar, clear jel and salt. Gradually add milk. Bring to a boil over medium heat, stirring constantly. Cook and stir for 2 minutes. Blend small amount of hot mixture into egg yolks. Mix well; return all to pan. Cook and stir for 2 minutes more. Remove from heat. Add butter and lemon juice. Set aside. Meringue: Beat egg whites until foamy. Add vanilla and cream of tartar. Beat until stiff. Gradually beat in sugar, until very stiff peaks form. Set aside. Fold sour cream into lemon mixture. Pour into a baked pie crust. Cover with meringue, sealing edges. Bake at 350° for 12-15 minutes or until golden. Cool and refrigerate.

Creamy Peanut Butter Pie

8 oz. cream cheese, softened
½ c. white sugar
⅓ c. creamy peanut butter
⅓ c. Cool Whip
10 peanut butter cups

Beat cream cheese, sugar and peanut butter until creamy. Fold in Cool Whip. Coarsely chop 5 peanut butter cups and stir into cream cheese mixture. Pour into 8" chocolate crumb crust. Quarter the remaining peanut butter cups; arrange on top. Refrigerate for 4 hours before cutting.

Frozen Peanut Butter Pie

3 oz. cream cheese, softened
1 c. powdered sugar
⅓ c. peanut butter
½ c. milk
2 c. Cool Whip
peanut butter cups

Beat cream cheese and powdered sugar until smooth. Add peanut butter and milk. Gently fold in Cool Whip. Pour into 8" graham cracker crust and freeze until firm. Serve with more Cool Whip and chopped peanut butter cups.

Peanut Butter Cup Pie

¾ c. white sugar
2 Tbsp. flour
1½ Tbsp. cocoa
⅓ c. milk
1 egg + 1 yolk, beaten
¾ tsp. vanilla

Topping:
4 oz. cream cheese, softened
¼ c. peanut butter
½ c. powdered sugar
1½ c. Cool Whip
½ tsp. vanilla
chocolate shavings

Combine sugar, flour and cocoa. Add milk, eggs and vanilla. Pour into 8" unbaked pie shell. Bake at 350° for 25-30 minutes or until set. Chill. Topping: Mix cream cheese, peanut butter and powdered sugar until smooth. Fold in Cool Whip and vanilla. Spread on top of chocolate layer. Top with more Cool Whip. Garnish with chocolate shavings.

Vanilla Sour Cream Pie

1 c. sour cream
1 c. milk
1 pkg. instant vanilla pudding

Beat sour cream and milk until smooth. Blend in pudding until smooth and slightly thickened. Pour into 8" graham cracker crust and chill for at least 1 hour or until set. Serve with Cool Whip.

Chocolate Cheese Pie

1 c. chocolate chips
8 oz. cream cheese, softened
¾ c. brown sugar, divided
⅛ tsp. salt
1 tsp. vanilla
2 eggs, separated
2 c. Cool Whip
chocolate shavings

Melt chocolate chips; set aside. Blend cream cheese, ½ c. brown sugar, salt and vanilla. Beat in egg yolks. Add chocolate; mix well. Beat egg whites until stiff. Gradually beat remaining ¼ c. sugar in until stiff. Fold chocolate mixture into egg whites. Pour into 9" baked pie shell. Chill until filling sets slightly. Top with Cool Whip. Garnish with chocolate shavings.

Chocolate Mousse Pie

1 (7 oz.) milk chocolate
   candy bar with almonds
16 lg. marshmallows or
   1½ c. mini marshmallows
½ c. milk
2 c. whipping cream, whipped

Place candy bar, marshmallows and milk in saucepan. Melt over low heat until smooth. Cool. Fold in whipped cream; pour into 8" baked pie shell, graham cracker crust or chocolate crumb crust. Chill for 3 hours.

Raspberry Cream Pie

½ c. raspberry juice
½ c. sweetened condensed milk
1 Tbsp. lemon juice
6 oz. Cool Whip

Mix all together with wire whip. Mix well; liquid settles in bottom. Pour into a baked pie shell. Refrigerate.

[H I N T]

When making meringue pies, be sure to spread meringue out to the edge of the crust. That way it won't pull up short during baking.

Pies

Basic Cream Pie Filling

2 c. milk
2 egg yolks
½ c. white sugar
2½ Tbsp. clear jel
½ tsp. salt
1 Tbsp. butter
1 tsp. vanilla

Scald 1½ c. milk. Mix remaining ½ c. milk with egg yolks. Add to scalding milk. Mix sugar, clear jel and salt; add to hot milk. Cook until thickened. Add butter and vanilla. Chill. For raisin cream pie: Add cooked raisins to cream filling. For coconut cream pie: Add ¾ c. coconut to hot pudding and chill. For peanut butter cream pie: Add ⅓ c. peanut butter to 1 c. powdered sugar for crumbs. For chocolate cream pie: Add 1 Tbsp. cocoa to hot pie filling and cool.

Two-Tone Cream Pie

¾ c. white sugar
½ c. clear jel
¼ tsp. salt
3 c. milk
3 egg yolks, beaten
2 Tbsp. butter
1 tsp. vanilla
2 Tbsp. peanut butter
1 oz. chocolate, melted

Meringue:
3 egg whites
¼ tsp. cream of tartar
5 Tbsp. white sugar
½ tsp. vanilla

In a saucepan, combine sugar, clear jel and salt. Gradually stir in milk. Cook and stir until thickened. Slowly add beaten egg yolks. Cook 2 minutes longer. Remove from heat; add butter and vanilla; chill. Divide mixture in half. Add peanut butter to half and melted chocolate to the other half. Spoon peanut butter mix into 9" baked pie crust. Top with chocolate layer. Meringue: Beat egg whites and cream of tartar until very stiff. Slowly add sugar and vanilla. Spread on top of pie, sealing edges. Bake at 400° for approximately 8-10 minutes or until golden.

Fresh Strawberry Pie

3 oz. cream cheese, softened
½ c. white sugar
½ tsp. vanilla
½ c. Cool Whip

Filling:
3 oz. strawberry Jell-O
¼ c. clear jel
¾ c. white sugar
¼ tsp. salt
1 c. water
1 c. 7-Up

1 qt. fresh strawberries, sliced

Mix cream cheese, sugar, vanilla and
Cool Whip until smooth. Spread
in bottom of baked 8" pie shell. Mix Jell-O,
clear jel, sugar and salt. Add water and
7-Up. Bring to a boil and cook until
clear. Cool and add fresh strawberries.
Pour filling over cream cheese layer in
crust. Top with Cool Whip.

Fresh Fruit Pie Filling

3 oz. Jell-O, raspberry, peach,
    strawberry, etc.
¼ c. clear jel
¾ c. white sugar
¼ tsp. salt
2 c. water
1 qt. fresh fruit
Cool Whip

Combine Jell-O, clear jel, sugar and salt.
Add water. Bring to a boil; cook until
clear. Cool; add fresh fruit. Put in
baked pie shell. Top with Cool Whip.

Large Batch Pie Dough Crumbs

10 c. Flaky Crust flour
¼ c. white sugar
1½ lb. butter Crisco
1½ tsp. baking powder
1 Tbsp. salt

Mix together to form crumbs. Keep in
a tight container. To use, add milk to
right consistency. Use approximately
1 c. crumbs for 1 (9") pie crust.

Pie Crust

3 c. Softex flour
pinch of salt
1¼ c. Crisco
1 egg
3 Tbsp. water
1 Tbsp. vinegar

Mix flour, salt and Crisco until crumbly. Beat egg, water and vinegar. Add to flour mixture; do not overmix. Let set for a few minutes. Makes 4 single or 2 double crusts.

Perfect Pie Crust

2 c. Flaky Crust flour
1½ tsp. white sugar
1 tsp. salt
½ tsp. baking powder
¾ c. Crisco
1½ tsp. vinegar
¼ c. cold water
1 egg yolk

Mix flour, sugar, salt, baking powder and Crisco until crumbly. Beat vinegar, water and egg yolk in a small bowl. Add to flour mixture and stir until moist.

Never-Fail Pie Crust

3 c. flour
1 tsp. salt
1¼ c. shortening
1 egg, beaten
1 Tbsp. vinegar
5 Tbsp. water

Cut shortening into flour and salt. Combine egg, vinegar and water. Pour liquid into flour mixture all at one time. Blend with a spoon, just until flour is moistened. Yield: 5 single pie crusts.

[H I N T]

If you're in a hurry to make a graham cracker crust, crush cinnamon graham crackers instead of plain ones. Since the cinnamon and sugar are already on the cracker, there's no need to add anything but melted butter.

Cakes and Frostings

At home when I was growing up, we had a strong sense of tradition about what should be on the table on Friday evenings. Pizza! When my siblings and I would walk in the door, coming home from school, Mom would be browning sausage for the pizza in her big frying pan. It was kind of a thank-God-it's-Friday moment, smelling that wonderful aroma.

Mom would even customize sections of the pizza to suit our individual tastes. Dad liked his without pepperoni and my youngest brother wasn't fond of onions, so they each got their own pieces just the way they liked them. We were all of the opinion that Mom's pizza couldn't be beat. That was our Friday evening menu for many years and I never grew tired of it!

—*Amy*

Sour Cream Coffee Cake

¼ c. butter, softened
½ c. white sugar
1 egg
1 c. flour
½ tsp. baking powder
¼ tsp. soda
½ c. sour cream

Cream butter and sugar. Add egg; beat well. Stir in flour, baking powder and soda. Add sour cream last. Pour into greased 8" baking dish. Mix topping ingredients and sprinkle on top of batter. Bake at 350° until toothpick comes out clean.

Topping:
⅓ c. chopped pecans
2 Tbsp. brown sugar
1 tsp. cinnamon

Yummy Sour Cream Coffee Cake

½ pkg. yellow cake mix
3 oz. instant vanilla pudding
2 eggs, beaten
½ c. sour cream
¼ c. vegetable oil
½ tsp. butter, melted
½ tsp. vanilla
½ tsp. cinnamon

Mix all ingredients together for cake and beat for 3-4 minutes. Pour half of the batter into a greased 8" square pan. In another bowl mix topping. Sprinkle half of topping on batter. Add rest of batter; sprinkle remaining topping on top. Bake at 350° for approximately 20 minutes or until toothpick comes out clean.

Topping:
2½ Tbsp. brown sugar
2½ Tbsp. white sugar
⅓ c. chopped pecans
½ tsp. cinnamon

Cakes and Frostings

Sour Cream Coffee Cake

½ c. butter, softened
1 c. white sugar
2 eggs, beaten
1 c. sour cream
1 tsp. baking soda
2 tsp. baking powder
pinch of salt
1 tsp. vanilla
2 c. flour

Topping:
¾ c. brown sugar
2 tsp. cinnamon
½ c. chopped nuts

Grease 8" springform pan with hole in middle. Sprinkle ⅓ of topping in bottom of pan. Add ½ of batter, ⅓ of topping and rest of batter and remaining topping. Bake at 350° for 50 minutes. Put pan on wire rack to cool. After 25 minutes remove from pan and invert onto plate.

[H I N T]

Chocolate Curls—Using a vegetable peeler, peel curls off a solid block of chocolate, allowing them to fall on a piece of waxed paper. If you get only shavings, warm the chocolate slightly. Slide a toothpick through each curl to gently lift it onto the cake.

Cream-Filled Coffee Cake

⅓ c. milk
⅓ stick butter
2½ Tbsp. white sugar
⅓ tsp. salt
1 sm. egg, beaten
½ Tbsp. yeast
2½ Tbsp. lukewarm water
1 c. + 2½ Tbsp. flour

Crumbs:
2 Tbsp. brown sugar
2 Tbsp. flour
⅓ tsp. cinnamon
2 tsp. cold butter
2½ Tbsp. chopped nuts

Filling:
¼ c. milk
2¼ tsp. flour
2½ Tbsp. Crisco
¼ c. white sugar
½ c. powdered sugar
¼ tsp. vanilla
½ c. + 2 Tbsp. marshmallow topping

Scald milk; add butter. When cooled add sugar, salt, egg, and yeast dissolved in warm water. Add flour. Mix all together and spoon into a greased 9" round cake pan. Mix crumb ingredients together. Sprinkle over batter. Let rise for 1-2 hours. Bake at 350° for 20 minutes or until done. Cool 15 minutes; remove from pan and cut in half. For filling, cook together milk and flour. Cool. Beat all ingredients together and spread on cake half. Top with other half.

Coffee Cake

½ c. milk
¼ c. butter
¼ c. white sugar
½ tsp. salt
1 egg, beaten
1½ tsp. yeast
1¾ c. flour

Crumbs:
2 Tbsp. brown sugar
2 Tbsp. flour
1½ Tbsp. butter, softened
½ tsp. cinnamon
¼ c. chopped nuts

Scald milk; add butter, sugar, salt and egg. Sprinkle yeast on top and dissolve. Mix in flour. Place in greased round pan. Mix crumbs; sprinkle on top of dough. Let rise for 30 minutes. Bake at 350° for 17-20 minutes. Fill with your favorite filling or use as strawberry shortcake.

Cherry Cheese Coffee Cake

8 oz. crescent rolls
8 oz. cream cheese, softened
⅓ c. powdered sugar
1 egg, separated
1 c. cherry pie filling

Press crescent rolls into greased 8" square baking dish, reserving 2 triangles. Bake at 350° for 10 minutes. Combine cream cheese, sugar and egg yolk. Spread over hot crust. Carefully spread cherry pie filling over it. Cut reserved triangles in half, roll into ropes and lay on top of filling, creating a lattice look. Beat egg white until soft peaks form; brush over dough. Bake another 18-20 minutes or until golden brown. Drizzle with powdered sugar glaze when cool.

Cherry Coffee Cake

½ c. butter, softened
¼ c. + 2 Tbsp. white sugar
¼ c. + 2 Tbsp. brown sugar
2 eggs
½ tsp. vanilla
1½ c. flour
¾ tsp. baking powder
¼ tsp. salt
1 c. cherry pie filling

Glaze:
¾ c. powdered sugar
¼ tsp. vanilla
1 Tbsp. butter, melted
warm milk to desired consistency

Cream butter and sugars. Add beaten eggs and vanilla. Sift and add dry ingredients. Spread ⅔ of dough in a 9" x 13" baking pan. Cover with pie filling. Spoon the rest of the dough in dabs over the top. Bake at 350° for 25-30 minutes or until baked. Drizzle with glaze while warm.

Early Bird Coffee Cake

1¼ c. flour
1 tsp. baking powder
¼ tsp. baking soda
¼ tsp. salt
¼ tsp. cinnamon
¼ tsp. nutmeg
1 c. brown sugar
⅓ c. shortening
¼ c. + 2 Tbsp. buttermilk
1 egg

Sift flour, baking powder, soda, salt, cinnamon and nutmeg into bowl. Cut in sugar and shortening. Remove ¼ c. + 2 Tbsp. for topping. Stir in milk and egg. Mix just until moistened. Grease a 9" round baking pan. Pour in batter and add topping. Bake at 350° for 25 minutes. Reduce heat to 325° and bake for approximately 15 minutes.

Moist Chocolate Cake

1 egg
½ c. brewed coffee, black
½ c. milk
¼ c. vegetable oil
1 tsp. vanilla
¼ tsp. salt
1 c. flour
1 c. white sugar
⅓ c. cocoa
1 tsp. baking powder
½ tsp. baking soda

Beat egg well; add all liquids and mix. Add dry ingredients. Batter will be thin. Pour into greased 8" or 9" square baking dish. Bake at 350° for 25-30 minutes or until toothpick comes out clean.

Jiffy Chocolate Cake

½ c. Crisco
1 c. white sugar
1 egg
½ c. buttermilk
½ c. boiling water
1 tsp. vanilla
1 tsp. baking soda
½ tsp. salt
2 c. flour
½ c. chocolate chips

Combine all ingredients in order given, except chocolate chips. Do not beat or mix until all ingredients are in bowl. Beat until well blended. Add chocolate chips. Bake in a greased 8" square pan at 350° for 25-30 minutes or until toothpick comes out clean.

Miracle Whip Cake

1 c. flour
½ c. white sugar
2 Tbsp. cocoa
1 tsp. baking soda
½ c. Miracle Whip
½ c. water
½ tsp. vanilla

Mix dry ingredients. Add Miracle Whip, water and vanilla. Pour into a greased 8" square baking pan. Bake at 350° until toothpick comes out clean. Frost with Crisco frosting (approximately half batch) found in this section.

Turtle Cake

½ pkg. chocolate cake mix
7 oz. caramels
6 Tbsp. butter
2 Tbsp. evaporated milk
½ c. chocolate chips

Mix cake mix as directed on package, using half the ingredients. Melt together caramels, butter and milk. Put half of cake mix in a greased 8" square baking dish. Bake until done. Pour chocolate chips on hot cake. Top with caramel sauce and the rest of the cake mix. Bake until done.

Chocolate Bavarian Torte

½ pkg. chocolate cake mix

Topping:
3 oz. cream cheese, softened
⅓ c. packed brown sugar
½ tsp. vanilla
pinch of salt
2 c. Cool Whip
grated chocolate

Mix cake mix according to package directions, using only half the ingredients. Bake in a greased 8" square pan at 350° until toothpick comes out clean. Cool. Beat cream cheese and brown sugar until creamy. Add vanilla, salt and Cool Whip. Spread on cake; sprinkle with chocolate shavings. Refrigerate.

[H I N T]

When you're making cupcakes, use a cookie scoop to place the batter in muffin cups.

Mocha Cream Torte

Crunch Layer:
¾ c. graham cracker crumbs
¼ c. + 2 Tbsp. brown sugar
¼ c. finely chopped nuts
1 Tbsp. instant coffee

Cake:
½ pkg. chocolate cake mix

Frosting:
4 oz. Cool Whip or
    ¾ c. Rich's topping, beaten
4 oz. cream cheese, softened
instant coffee to taste
3 tsp. white sugar

Place crunch layer in a greased 9" x 11" pan. Mix cake mix according to package directions, using only half the ingredients. Pour cake batter in pan. Bake at 350° until toothpick comes out clean. Beat frosting ingredients and place on top of cake when cooled. Refrigerate.

Chocolate Praline Cake

½ pkg. chocolate cake mix
¼ c. butter
2 Tbsp. whipping cream
½ c. packed brown sugar
⅓ c. chopped pecans

Combine butter, whipping cream and brown sugar. Cook over low heat just until butter is melted, stirring occasionally. Pour into a greased 8" square pan. Sprinkle pecans evenly on top. Mix cake mix according to package directions, using only half the ingredients. Pour over pecan layer. Bake at 325° until toothpick comes out clean. Cool 5 minutes; invert onto a serving plate. Cool. Top with Cool Whip. Garnish with chopped pecans or chocolate curls.

Ho-Ho Cake

½ pkg. chocolate cake mix

Topping:
2½ Tbsp. flour
⅔ c. milk
¼ c. butter, softened
½ c. Crisco
½ tsp. vanilla
½ c. white sugar

Icing:
¼ c. butter
2½ Tbsp. cocoa
1 egg yolk
½ tsp. vanilla
1½ Tbsp. hot water
1½ c. powdered sugar

Mix cake mix according to package directions, using half the ingredients. Bake in an 8" square pan. Cook together flour and milk. Cream together remaining topping ingredients and beat well. Add cooled flour mixture and beat again. Spread on cooled cake. Melt butter; add cocoa. Remove from heat. Beat egg yolk, vanilla and hot water. Add to butter. Add sifted powdered sugar and blend well. Spread over topping. You might have to add more hot water if it doesn't spread easily. Refrigerate.

Hot Fudge Sundae Cake

¾ c. white sugar
2 tsp. vegetable oil
½ c. milk
1 tsp. vanilla
2 tsp. cocoa
¼ tsp. salt
2 tsp. baking powder
1 c. flour
1 c. chopped nuts
¾ c. brown sugar
¼ c. cocoa
1⅓ c. hot water

Mix first 9 ingredients well and pour into a greased 8" square pan. Sprinkle brown sugar and cocoa on top of batter. Pour hot water over top to make sauce. Bake at 350° for 40 minutes.

Self-Filled Cupcakes

½ pkg. chocolate cake mix

Filling:
3 oz. cream cheese, softened
¼ c. white sugar
1 egg yolk

Prepare cake mix according to package directions, using half the ingredients. Mix filling ingredients until smooth. Fill greased cupcake tins half full with cake batter. Put 1 Tbsp. cream cheese mixture on top. Bake at 350° until toothpick comes out clean.

Moist Brownies

1 c. flour
1 c. white sugar
2 Tbsp. cocoa
¼ c. vegetable oil
¼ c. butter
½ c. water
1 egg, beaten
⅛ tsp. salt
¼ c. buttermilk or milk
½ tsp. baking soda
½ tsp. vanilla

mini marshmallows

Frosting:
¼ c. butter
2 Tbsp. cocoa
3 Tbsp. milk
powdered sugar

Put flour and sugar in mixing bowl. Boil cocoa, oil, butter and water together in saucepan. Pour over sugar and flour mixture. Stir. Add egg, salt, buttermilk, baking soda and vanilla. Mix together and pour into a greased 8" square pan. Bake at 300° until toothpick comes out clean. Remove from oven and sprinkle with a layer of mini marshmallows. Return to oven for 3 minutes. Remove and cool. Boil butter, cocoa and milk for 1 minute. Remove from heat. Add powdered sugar until spreading consistency. Spread over brownies.

Texas Sheet Cake

¼ c. butter
¼ c. water
1 Tbsp. cocoa
½ c. white sugar
½ c. flour
¼ tsp. vanilla
1 egg yolk
2 Tbsp. sour cream or milk
⅛ tsp. salt
¼ tsp. baking soda

Icing:
2 Tbsp. butter
1 Tbsp. cocoa
1½ Tbsp. milk
¼ lb. powdered sugar
¼ tsp. vanilla
chopped nuts

Melt butter in saucepan. Add water and cocoa. Bring to a boil. Remove from heat and add remaining ingredients. Pour into a greased 8" square pan. Bake at 350° until toothpick comes out clean. Boil together butter, cocoa and milk. Remove from heat; add powdered sugar and vanilla. Spread on cake while warm. Sprinkle nuts on top.

[H I N T]

When icing a layer cake, slide three dry stick spaghetti through the layers to prevent them from sliding before the icing sets.

Cakes and Frostings

Peanut Butter Flan Cake

½ pkg. chocolate cake mix

Topping:
3 oz. cream cheese, softened
¼ c. peanut butter
1½ tsp. white sugar
½ tsp. vanilla
⅔ c. milk
⅓ c. instant vanilla pudding
2¼ c. Cool Whip, divided
Reese's peanut butter cups

Prepare cake mix according to package directions, using half the ingredients. Pour into a greased flan pan or an 8" square pan. Bake at 350° until toothpick comes out clean. If you're using a flan pan, cool for 10 minutes, then invert onto a serving plate. Cream together cream cheese and peanut butter. Add sugar and vanilla. Whisk milk and pudding. Let set until thickened. Fold in peanut butter mixture. Stir in 1½ c. Cool Whip. Spread on cake. Top with remaining Cool Whip. Cut peanut butter cups into wedges. Set up in whipped topping. Refrigerate.

Peanut Butter Candy Cake

¾ c. boiling water
¼ c. butter
½ c. oatmeal
½ c. brown sugar
½ c. white sugar
1 egg
¾ c. all-purpose flour
½ tsp. baking soda
¼ tsp. baking powder
⅛ tsp. salt
⅛ tsp. cinnamon
chocolate chips
chopped peanut butter cups

Combine water, butter and oatmeal. Let cool before adding other ingredients. Mix sugars with oatmeal mixture. Add egg. In a bowl put flour, soda, baking powder, salt and cinnamon. Mix; add to rest of ingredients. Pour into a greased 8" square pan. Bake at 350° for 20-25 minutes or until toothpick comes out clean. Sprinkle with chocolate chips and chopped peanut butter cups.

Oatmeal Chocolate Chip Cake

¾ c. + 2 Tbsp. boiling water
½ c. uncooked quick oats
¼ c. butter
½ c. brown sugar
½ c. white sugar
1 egg
¾ c. + 2 Tbsp. flour
½ tsp. baking soda
¼ tsp. salt
½ Tbsp. cocoa
6 oz. chocolate chips
chopped nuts

Pour boiling water over oatmeal. Let set for 10 minutes. Add butter and sugars. Stir until butter is melted. Add egg and mix well. Sift and add dry ingredients. Mix well. Add about half of chocolate chips. Pour batter into a greased 8" square pan. Sprinkle nuts and remaining chocolate chips on top. Bake at 350° for approximately 30 minutes.

Yellow Pound Cake

1 pkg. yellow cake mix
1 pkg. instant vanilla pudding
⅓ c. vegetable oil
4 eggs
1 c. water

Glaze:
1½ c. powdered sugar
1 tsp. vanilla
2 Tbsp. butter, melted
warm milk to right consistency

Blend all ingredients in a large bowl. Beat at medium speed for 2 minutes. Grease and flour a tube pan. Bake at 350° for 50-60 minutes or until toothpick comes out clean. Cool in pan for 25 minutes, then invert onto plate. Frost with glaze when cooled. You can also use lemon or chocolate cake mixes and puddings for different flavors.

Cakes and Frostings

Yellow Whipped Cream Cake

¾ c. chilled whipped cream
2 sm. eggs
¾ tsp. vanilla
1 c. +2 Tbsp. cake flour
¾ c. white sugar
1 tsp. baking powder
¼ tsp. salt

Preheat oven to 350°. Beat cream until stiff. Beat eggs until thick and lemon colored. Fold eggs and vanilla into whipped cream. Combine dry ingredients. Fold into cream mixture. Pour into a greased 8" square pan. Bake until toothpick comes out clean.

Graham Streusel Cake

½ pkg. yellow cake mix
½ c. water
2 Tbsp. vegetable oil
1 egg

Crumbs:
½ pkg. graham crackers, crushed
1½ tsp. cinnamon
¼ c. butter, melted
½ c. brown sugar

Glaze:
powdered sugar
warm milk or water
    to desired consistency
vanilla

Mix together with a beater for 2 minutes. Pour into a greased 8" square baking dish. Mix crumbs together and sprinkle over batter. Swirl with a knife. Bake at 350° for 20-25 minutes or until toothpick comes out clean. Drizzle with powdered sugar glaze.

Blueberry Pound Cake

½ c. butter, softened
1½ c. white sugar
¾ tsp. vanilla
¼ tsp. lemon extract
3 eggs
1½ c. flour
⅛ tsp. baking soda
½ c. sour cream
1½ c. fresh or frozen blueberries

Cream butter and sugar; add extracts. Add eggs one at a time, beating well. Combine flour and baking soda. Add to creamed mixture alternately with sour cream. Fold in blueberries. Spoon into greased, waxed paper lined 9" x 5" loaf pan. Bake at 350° for 45-55 minutes or until toothpick comes out clean. Serve with warm blueberry pie filling if desired.

Blueberry Buckle

6 Tbsp. butter, softened
½ c. white sugar
1 egg
1 tsp. vanilla
1 tsp. lemon juice
½ c. milk
2 c. flour
2 tsp. baking powder
1 c. fresh or frozen blueberries

Cream butter and sugar. Beat in egg, vanilla and lemon juice. Stir in milk. Fold in dry ingredients. Add blueberries and spread batter in a greased 8" square pan. Combine crumb ingredients until crumbly. Sprinkle over batter and bake at 375° for 30 minutes or until toothpick comes out clean. Serve warm with milk.

Crumbs:
⅓ c. flour
¼ c. butter
¼ c. white sugar
¼ c. brown sugar

Cakes and Frostings

Angel Food Cake from Scratch

1 c. sifted cake flour
¾ c. white sugar
1½ c. egg whites
1½ tsp. cream of tartar
¼ tsp. salt
1½ tsp. vanilla
¾ c. white sugar

Sift flour with ¾ c. sugar. Beat egg whites with cream of tartar, salt and vanilla until stiff peaks form. Add the remaining ¾ c. sugar, 2 Tbsp. at a time. Continue beating until meringue holds peaks. Fold in flour mixture by fourths. Bake in ungreased 10" tube pan at 375° for 35-40 minutes or until done. Invert pan and let cool.

Toffee Angel Cake

2 slices angel food cake
Cool Whip
caramel ice cream topping
toffee bits

Place each cake slice on a serving plate. Put a dab of Cool Whip on top. Drizzle with caramel topping. Sprinkle with toffee bits.

Alaska Sheet Cake

¼ c. butter
¼ c. water
½ c. white sugar
¼ tsp. salt
¼ tsp. baking soda
⅔ c. flour
1 sm. egg
2 Tbsp. buttermilk

Frosting:
2 Tbsp. butter
¾ Tbsp. milk
¼ lb. powdered sugar
¼ tsp. vanilla
nuts, optional

Bring butter and water to a boil. Remove from heat and stir until butter is melted. Add dry ingredients; mix well. Add egg and buttermilk. Pour into a greased 8" or 9" square pan. Bake at 350° until toothpick comes out clean. Bring butter and milk to a boil and add powdered sugar and vanilla. Spread frosting on cake while still warm. Sprinkle with chopped nuts.

Jell-O Cake

½ pkg. white cake mix
3 Tbsp. strawberry or
   raspberry Jell-O
½ c. boiling water
½ c. powdered sugar
3 oz. cream cheese, softened
¾ c. Cool Whip

Fruit Filling:
½ c. white sugar
3 Tbsp. strawberry or
   raspberry Jell-O
2 Tbsp. clear jel
1 c. water
1-1½ c. fresh strawberries
   or raspberries

Prepare cake mix according to package directions, using half the ingredients. Bake in an 8" square pan at 350° until a toothpick comes out clean. Poke holes in cake with fork. Dissolve Jell-O in boiling water. Pour over warm cake. Cool. Mix powdered sugar and cream cheese; add Cool Whip. Spread on top of cooled cake. Mix sugar, Jell-O and clear jel in a saucepan. Add water. Bring to a boil and cook until clear. Cool and add fresh strawberries or raspberries. Spread over cream cheese layer on cake. Chill.

Lemon Cake

½ pkg. lemon cake mix
⅓ c. lime Jell-O
¾ c. boiling water
⅓ c. instant lemon pudding
¾ c. milk
¼ c. Cool Whip

Mix cake mix according to package directions, using half the ingredients. Bake in an 8" square baking dish. Poke holes in cake with a fork while still hot. Dissolve Jell-O in boiling water. Pour over cake. Refrigerate cake. Mix lemon pudding with milk. Fold in Cool Whip. Spread over cake. Refrigerate until serving.

Carrot Cake

1 c. white sugar
½ c. + 2 Tbsp. vegetable oil
2 eggs
1 c. flour
1 tsp. baking soda
½ tsp. salt
1 tsp. cinnamon
1½ c. raw shredded carrots
¼ c. chopped nuts

Cream Cheese Frosting:
2 oz. cream cheese, softened
2 Tbsp. butter, softened
¼ lb. powdered sugar
¼ tsp. vanilla
chopped nuts

Cream sugar and oil. Add eggs; beat well. Sift flour, soda, salt and cinnamon together and add to creamed mixture. Fold in carrots and nuts. Bake at 350° for approximately 45 minutes or until toothpick comes out clean. Frost with cream cheese frosting. Sprinkle with nuts.

Blue Ribbon Banana Cake

⅓ c. butter, softened
¾ c. white sugar
1 egg, beaten
½ c. mashed bananas
¼ c. buttermilk
1 c. flour
½ tsp. baking powder
½ tsp. baking soda
½ tsp. vanilla
¼ c. coconut
¼ c. chopped nuts

Cream butter and sugar. Add egg, bananas and buttermilk. Stir in flour, baking powder, soda, vanilla, coconut and nuts. Bake in a greased 8" square pan at 350° for 30 minutes or until toothpick comes out clean. Frost with cream cheese icing.

Apple Cake

1 egg
1 c. white sugar
¼ c. vegetable oil
½ tsp. vanilla
⅛ tsp. salt
1 tsp. baking soda
1 tsp. cinnamon
1 c. flour
2 c. diced apples
½ c. chopped nuts

Frosting:
3 oz. cream cheese, softened
1½ Tbsp. butter, melted
¾ c. powdered sugar
½ tsp. vanilla

Cream egg and sugar; add rest of ingredients and stir well. Pour into a greased 8" square pan. Bake at 350° for 30 minutes or until toothpick comes out clean. Mix frosting ingredients well. Spread on cake.

Sour Cream Peach Kuchen

1½ c. flour
¼ c. white sugar, divided
¼ tsp. baking powder
⅛ tsp. salt
½ c. cold butter
3 c. canned peach slices, drained
½ tsp. cinnamon

Topping:
2 egg yolks
1 c. sour cream
1 Tbsp. white sugar
⅛ tsp. cinnamon

Combine flour, ⅛ c. sugar, baking powder and salt. Cut in butter until crumbly. Press into bottom and up sides of a greased 8" square pan. Arrange peaches over crust. Combine ½ tsp. cinnamon and remaining sugar. Sprinkle over peaches. Bake at 400° for 15 minutes. Combine egg yolks and sour cream; spread over peaches. Mix 1 Tbsp. sugar and ⅛ tsp. cinnamon. Sprinkle on top. Bake 25-30 minutes longer until golden. Serve warm or cold.

Cakes and Frostings

Jelly Roll

4 eggs
1 tsp. vanilla
1 c. white sugar
1 c. cake flour
¼ tsp. salt
1 tsp. baking powder
3 tsp. cocoa, optional

Beat eggs and vanilla until thick and lemon-colored. Gradually beat in sugar until mixture is fluffy and thick. Sift dry ingredients and add all at once. Fold in or beat on low. Line a 10" x 15" jelly roll pan with waxed paper. Use shortening underneath and on waxed paper. Bake at 375° for 15 minutes or at 350° for 30 minutes. Dust a clean tea towel with powdered sugar. Invert cake onto towel. Roll up with towel. Cool on rack. Unroll; fill with ice cream or favorite filling. Roll up again.

Pumpkin Roll

1 c. white sugar
¾ c. flour
1 tsp. salt
1 tsp. cinnamon
3 eggs
⅔ c. pumpkin
¾ c. chopped nuts, optional

Filling:
2 tsp. butter, softened
8 oz. cream cheese, softened
1 tsp. vanilla
1 c. powdered sugar

Mix dry ingredients. Add eggs and pumpkin. Grease a cookie sheet and line with waxed paper. Sprinkle with nuts if desired. Bake at 350° for approximately 15 minutes. Cool for 5 minutes; flip onto tea towel sprinkled with powdered sugar. Remove waxed paper immediately and roll in tea towel. Cool. Mix all filling ingredients until creamy. Unroll cake and spread with cream cheese filling. Reroll, starting at short end. Refrigerate. Wait at least 1 hour before cutting.

Crisco Frosting

⅓ c. water
¼ tsp. salt
½ tsp. clear vanilla
3 c. powdered sugar
⅔ c. Crisco

Beat all ingredients until light and fluffy.

Caramel Frosting

¾ c. butter
1 c. brown sugar
½ c. milk
3 c. powdered sugar

Bring butter and brown sugar to a boil. Boil for 2-3 minutes, stirring constantly. Add milk and bring to a boil; remove from heat and cool completely. Stir in powdered sugar.

Cream Cheese Frosting

3 oz. cream cheese, softened
6 Tbsp. butter, melted
1 tsp. vanilla
1 tsp. milk
2½ c. powdered sugar

Mix all ingredients until smooth and creamy.

Creamy Chocolate Frosting

2½ Tbsp. butter, softened
1½ c. powdered sugar
2 Tbsp. cocoa
1 tsp. vanilla
1½-2 Tbsp. milk
1¼ tsp. instant coffee, optional

Mix until smooth and fluffy. Add coffee with the powdered sugar for creamy mocha frosting.

Cakes and Frostings

Vanilla Butter Cream Frosting

1½ c. powdered sugar
2½ Tbsp. butter, softened
¾ tsp. vanilla
½-1 Tbsp. milk

Mix powdered sugar and butter; stir in vanilla and add milk gradually until frosting is smooth and spreadable. For lemon butter cream frosting, omit vanilla, substitute lemon juice for milk and add ¼ tsp. grated lemon peel. For orange butter cream frosting, omit vanilla, substitute orange juice for milk and add 1 tsp. grated orange peel.

Sour Cream Frosting

¼ c. butter
¾ c. brown sugar
1 tsp. vanilla
½ c. sour cream
1 tsp. milk
powdered sugar, optional

Cook butter, brown sugar, vanilla, sour cream and milk for 3 minutes. Cool. Add powdered sugar if it is too thin.

Cookies

Here is a memory and a recipe that one of my aunts shared with me: We would go through Grandpas' part of the house in the evening on our way to the stairway leading up to our bedroom. We never felt quite right going to bed without saying good night to them. We felt loved by our grandparents! As we passed through their kitchen, often they had a jelly dish sitting on the table filled with elderberry honey, a favorite of mine. Here is the recipe.

Elderberry Honey

4 c. elderberry juice

4 c. Karo

3 c. white sugar

Cook all ingredients together until the desired consistency is obtained.

—Sam

Just-Right Chocolate Chip Cookies

⅔ c. butter
⅔ c. butter Crisco
¾ c. white sugar
¾ c. brown sugar
2 eggs
1 tsp. vanilla
1 tsp. soda
1 tsp. salt
⅓ c. instant vanilla pudding
3 c. flour
12 oz. chocolate chips

Bake at 350° for 14-18 minutes. Do not overbake.

Chocolate Chip Cookies

¾ c. butter, softened
½ c. Crisco
¾ c. brown sugar
¾ c. white sugar
2 eggs
⅔ c. instant vanilla pudding
2 tsp. vanilla
1 tsp. soda
1 tsp. salt
3 c. flour
1¾ c. milk chocolate chips

Cream butter, Crisco and sugars. Add eggs, instant pudding, vanilla, soda and salt. Mix well. Add flour and chocolate chips. Roll into balls and bake at 350° until lightly browned. Do not overbake.

[H I N T]

To make uniform impressions in delicate thumbprint cookies, use a small extract bottle. Press the bottle with the cap in place into the cookies and twist. Fill as desired.

Cookies

Choc-Oat-Chip Cookies

½ c. butter-flavored Crisco
¼ c. white sugar
⅔ c. brown sugar
1 egg
1 Tbsp. milk
1 tsp. vanilla
1 c. flour
½ tsp. soda
¼ tsp. salt
1¼ c. oatmeal
1 c. chocolate chips
½ c. chopped nuts

Beat Crisco and sugars until creamy. Add egg, milk and vanilla. Beat well. Add flour, soda and salt. Mix well. Add remaining ingredients. Bake at 350° for 10-12 minutes.

Original Toll House Cookies

½ c. butter, softened
¼ c. + 2 Tbsp. white sugar
¼ c. + 2 Tbsp. brown sugar
¼ tsp. water
½ tsp. vanilla
1 egg
1¼ c. + 2 Tbsp. flour
½ tsp. salt
½ tsp. soda
6 oz. mini chocolate chips

Sift together dry ingredients; set aside. Beat butter, sugars, water and vanilla until creamy. Add egg and mix well. Add dry ingredients; mix well. Add chocolate chips. Chill dough. On a floured surface roll dough in ½" ropes. Slice off ¼" slices and bake at 350° until lightly browned.

Outrageous Chocolate Chip Cookies

¾ c. butter, softened
1 c. white sugar
⅔ c. brown sugar
2 eggs
1 c. peanut butter
1 tsp. vanilla
2 c. flour
2 tsp. soda
¼ tsp. salt
1 c. oatmeal
1½ c. chocolate chips

Cream butter and sugars; beat in eggs, peanut butter and vanilla. Add dry ingredients and chocolate chips. Drop by tsp. on ungreased cookie sheets. Bake at 350° until golden brown. Cool for 1 minute before removing from pan.

Chocolate Chip Debbies

¾ c. shortening
1⅓ c. brown sugar
2 eggs
1 tsp. vanilla
1 c. + 2 Tbsp. flour
¾ tsp. soda
½ tsp. cinnamon
½ tsp. salt
2 c. oatmeal
¾ c. chocolate chips

Cream together shortening and sugar. Beat eggs and vanilla; add to shortening mixture. Put flour, soda, cinnamon, salt, oatmeal and chocolate chips in a bowl. Stir into batter. Drop onto greased cookie sheets. Bake at 350° until golden brown. Take out of oven and let set a few minutes before removing from pan. Blend filling ingredients well and spread between two cookies.

Filling:
¾ c. shortening
3 c. powdered sugar
¾ c. + 2 Tbsp. marshmallow
   topping
3 Tbsp. milk or to spreading
   consistency

Cookies

Neiman's $250 Chocolate Chip Cookies

1 c. butter
1 c. brown sugar
1 c. white sugar
2 eggs
½ tsp. salt
2½ c. oatmeal
2 c. flour
1 tsp. baking powder
1 tsp. baking soda
1 tsp. vanilla
12 oz. chocolate chips
½ c. chopped nuts
8 oz. chocolate bar, grated

Cream butter, sugars and eggs. Add remaining dry ingredients. Add vanilla. Stir in chocolate chips, nuts and chocolate bar. Roll in walnut size balls. Bake at 350° for 10 minutes or until lightly browned.

Easy Peanut Butter Jumbos

1½ c. peanut butter
½ c. butter, softened
1 c. white sugar
1 c. brown sugar
3 eggs
1 tsp. vanilla
4 c. oatmeal
2 tsp. baking soda
1 c. chocolate chips
1 c. M&M's

Drop by Tbsp. on ungreased cookie sheets. Bake at 350° for 12-14 minutes or until slightly brown. Do not overbake.

[HINT]

A pizza cutter makes cutting brownies a breeze. You can cut the pieces more evenly and the brownies won't stick to the cutter. It works well with fudge, too.

Monster Cookies

½ c. shortening
1 c. white sugar
1 c. brown sugar
3 eggs
¾ tsp. vanilla
¾ tsp. corn syrup
1¾ c. peanut butter
2 tsp. baking soda
4 c. oatmeal
¾ c. flour
¾ c. chocolate chips
¾ c. M&M's

Mix together and chill. Form into balls and roll in powdered sugar. Bake at 350° for 15 minutes.

Triple Treat Cookies

½ c. butter, softened
¾ c. brown sugar
¾ c. white sugar
½ c. peanut butter
2 eggs
2 tsp. baking soda
1 tsp. salt
2¼ c. flour
1 c. chocolate chips

Filling:
½ c. peanut butter
2 Tbsp. butter, softened
⅓ c. milk
1 tsp. vanilla
2-3 c. powdered sugar

Make balls and bake at 350°. Do not overbake. Spread filling between two cookies.

Mom's Peanut Butter Crisscrosses

1½ c. shortening
1½ c. brown sugar
1½ c. white sugar
1½ c. peanut butter
3 eggs
1½ tsp. vanilla
3 tsp. baking soda
¾ tsp. salt
3¾ c. + 2 Tbsp. flour

Form into small balls. Put on ungreased baking sheets. Press with a potato masher or fork. Bake at 350°. Do not overbake.

Rob Roy Cookies

1 c. shortening
1½ c. brown sugar
¼ c. buttermilk
2 eggs
1 tsp. salt
½ tsp. cloves
¾ tsp. baking soda
½ tsp. cinnamon
1¾ c. flour
1½ c. oatmeal
1 c. nuts, optional
1 c. raisins, optional

Combine shortening, sugar, milk and eggs; beat well. Add dry ingredients to shortening mixture, then add oatmeal, nuts and raisins. Drop by tsp. onto greased baking sheets. Bake at 375° for 10-15 minutes. Makes approximately 3 dozen.

Winter Energy Cookies

1 c. butter
1½ c. brown sugar
⅓ c. molasses
⅓ c. peanut butter
2 lg. eggs
1½ tsp. vanilla
1½ c. whole wheat flour
1 c. white flour
1 c. wheat germ
1½ tsp. baking soda
½ tsp. salt
½ tsp. cinnamon
2 c. oatmeal
1 c. raisins
1 c. chocolate chips
1 c. chopped walnuts or peanuts

Cream butter, sugar, molasses and peanut butter in a large bowl. Blend in the eggs and vanilla. Mix the flours, wheat germ, baking soda, salt and cinnamon in a separate bowl. Stir the dry ingredients into the creamed mixture until evenly blended. Stir in oatmeal, raisins, chocolate chips and nuts. Cover and refrigerate for 1 hour. Preheat oven to 350° and lightly grease baking sheets. Shape dough into balls, using ¼ c. dough per cookie. Place on sheets, leaving 3" between them. Flatten slightly with a fork. Bake for 15-18 minutes. When done the tops will still be soft to touch. Cool on sheets for 5 minutes, then transfer to a rack to cool. Makes 2 dozen large cookies.

[H I N T]

When a recipe calls for chocolate kisses, use chocolate stars instead. They are less expensive, prettier and you won't have to spend the time unwrapping them.

Spellbinder Cookies

1½ c. flour
1½ tsp. baking powder
1 tsp. baking soda
1 c. brown sugar
1 c. butter, softened
1 egg
1 c. oatmeal
1 c. coconut, optional
½ c. crushed cornflakes

Icing:
2 Tbsp. butter, melted
1 Tbsp. hot water
1 c. powdered sugar
1 tsp. vanilla

Combine flour, baking powder and soda. Gradually add sugar to butter in a mixing bowl. Cream well. Add egg; beat well. Gradually add dry ingredients, blending well after each addition. Stir in oatmeal, coconut and cornflakes. Make rounded tsp. sized balls. Roll in additional crushed cornflakes. Bake on ungreased cookie sheets. Flatten balls slightly. Bake at 375°. Dab icing onto cookies.

Double Chocolate Jumbo Crisps

½ c. + 2 Tbsp. butter, softened
¾ c. white sugar
1 sm. egg
½ tsp. vanilla
3 Tbsp. cocoa
¼ tsp. baking soda
¼ tsp. salt
2 Tbsp. hot water
¾ c. flour
1½ c. oatmeal
½ c. chocolate chips

Filling:
1 egg white, beaten
¾ c. shortening
1½ tsp. vanilla
1 c. powdered sugar

Cream butter and sugar; beat in egg, vanilla, cocoa, soda and salt. Stir in hot water, flour, oatmeal and chocolate chips. Drop by teaspoons onto ungreased baking sheets. Bake at 350° for 15 minutes. When cool, spread filling between 2 cookies.

Chocolate Gobs

2 c. white sugar
1 c. shortening
2 eggs, beaten
4 c. flour
2 tsp. salt
½ c. cocoa
1 c. sour milk or buttermilk
1 c. hot water
2 tsp. baking soda

Filling:
2 egg whites, beaten
4 tsp. flour
4 c. powdered sugar, divided
4 tsp. milk
4 tsp. vanilla
1½ c. shortening

Blend sugar and shortening; add beaten eggs. Sift flour, salt and cocoa. Alternate flour mixture with milk. At the end add hot water and soda mixture. Drop onto cookie sheets; flatten with spoon dipped in water. Bake at 375°. When cool, spread filling between two cookies. These cookies freeze well. Can also be filled with ice cream instead of filling, then frozen. For filling, beat together egg whites, flour, 2 c. powdered sugar, milk and vanilla. Add shortening and 2 c. powdered sugar. Blend until smooth.

Peanut Butter Blossoms

1 c. white sugar
1 c. brown sugar
1 c. butter
1 c. peanut butter
2 eggs
¼ c. milk
2 tsp. vanilla
3½ c. flour
2 tsp. baking soda
1 tsp. salt
Hershey's kisses

Cream sugars, butter and peanut butter together. Beat eggs, milk and vanilla. Sift flour, soda and salt; stir into batter. Chill thoroughly. Shape into balls the size of a walnut, then roll in additional white sugar. Bake on ungreased cookie sheets at 350°. Press chocolate Hershey's kisses in centers while still hot.

Cookies

Mountain Cookies

½ c. butter, softened
½ c. powdered sugar
1 tsp. vanilla
1 c. flour
¼ tsp. salt

Filling:
1½ oz. cream cheese, softened
½ c. powdered sugar
1 Tbsp. flour
½ tsp. vanilla
¼ c. finely chopped pecans
¼ c. coconut

Topping:
¼ c. chocolate chips
1 Tbsp. butter or margarine
1 Tbsp. water
¼ c. powdered sugar

Cream butter, sugar and vanilla. Combine flour and salt. Gradually add to creamed mixture. Shape into 1" balls. Place 2" apart on ungreased cookie sheet. Make a deep indentation in the center of each ball. Bake at 350° for 10-12 minutes or until edges start to brown. Remove and cool completely. For filling, beat cream cheese, sugar, flour and vanilla. Add pecans and coconut. Mix well. Spoon ½ tsp. in each cookie. For topping, heat chocolate chips, butter and water in a saucepan until melted. Add sugar. Drizzle over cookies.

Oatmeal Chewies

1 c. butter, softened
2 c. brown sugar
2 eggs
1 tsp. vanilla
1½ c. flour
3 c. oatmeal
1 tsp. baking powder
1 tsp. baking soda
½ tsp. salt
2 c. chocolate chips

Mix all together. Chill dough; make balls and roll in powdered sugar. Bake at 350° until lightly browned.

Drop Oatmeal Cookies

1¼ c. butter
2¼ c. brown sugar
3 eggs
1½ tsp. vanilla
3 c. oatmeal
2½ c. flour
1⅛ tsp. soda
¾ tsp. salt
1½ tsp. cinnamon

Filling:
2 c. powdered sugar
¾ c. shortening
1 tsp. vanilla

Bake at 350° until lightly browned. Do not overbake. Mix powdered sugar, shortening and vanilla together and fold in 2 beaten egg whites. Spread filling between 2 cookies.

Butterscotch Crunch Cookies

1 c. shortening
1 c. brown sugar
1 c. white sugar
2 eggs
1 tsp. vanilla
1½ c. flour
1 tsp. salt
1 tsp. baking soda
3 c. oatmeal

Mix well and bake at 400° for 10 minutes. Do not overbake. Ice with brown sugar icing if desired.

Caramel Cookies

½ c. butter
2 c. brown sugar
2 eggs
1 Tbsp. water
2 tsp. vanilla
2 tsp. baking soda
1 tsp. cream of tartar
3¼ c. flour

Mix together and shape into rolls. Refrigerate overnight. Cut into ½" slices and bake at 350°.

Orange Jell-O Cookies

½ c. white sugar
⅓ c. orange Jell-O
1 c. butter
2 eggs
1 tsp. vanilla
2¾ c. flour
1 tsp. soda
½ tsp. salt
½ c. milk

Frosting:
butter
milk
powdered sugar
orange extract

Cream together sugar, Jell-O and butter. Add beaten eggs and vanilla. Alternate dry ingredients with milk, ending with dry ingredients. Drop by tsp. onto ungreased cookie sheets. Bake at 375°.

Soft Sugar Cutout Cookies

1 c. white sugar
½ c. butter
½ tsp. vanilla
1 egg
2½ c. flour
1 tsp. baking powder
1 tsp. baking soda
¼ tsp. salt
1 c. buttermilk

Frosting:
1½ Tbsp. butter, melted
powdered sugar
½ tsp. vanilla
milk to desired consistency

Mix sugar, butter and vanilla. Add beaten egg. Mix together dry ingredients. Alternate buttermilk and dry ingredients, ending with dry ingredients. Chill for a few hours. Roll out on floured surface until ¼" thick. Cut with your favorite cookie cutters. Bake on greased baking sheet at 375° for 8-12 minutes. Frost and decorate cookies as desired.

Pumpkin Cookies

¾ c. shortening
1½ c. brown sugar
1½ c. pumpkin
2 sm. eggs, beaten
3 c. flour
1½ tsp. baking powder
1¼ tsp. baking soda
1½ tsp. cinnamon
¾ c. chopped nuts, optional
¾ c. raisins, optional

Orange Icing:
1½ c. powdered sugar
¾ Tbsp. butter, melted
orange juice to desired consistency

Cream shortening and sugar; add pumpkin and eggs. Mix well. Add dry ingredients. Add nuts and raisins. Drop by Tbsp. on greased baking sheets. Bake at 350°.

Cookies

Pumpkin Whoopie Pie Cookies

1¾ c. brown sugar
1 c. vegetable oil
2 eggs
1½ c. pumpkin
1 tsp. vanilla
3 c. flour
1 tsp. baking powder
1 tsp. baking soda
1½ tsp. cinnamon
1 tsp. salt

Filling:
3 oz. cream cheese, softened
¼ c. butter, softened
½ tsp. vanilla
3 c. powdered sugar

Cream sugar and oil; add eggs, pumpkin and vanilla. Blend well. Add dry ingredients and mix well. Drop by tsp. onto cookie sheet and flatten slightly. Bake at 350° for 10-12 minutes. Cream together filling ingredients and spread between 2 cookies.

Cream Wafer Cookies

½ c. butter, softened
1 c. brown sugar
2 eggs
1 tsp. vanilla
3 Tbsp. cream or Rich's topping
2½-2¾ c. flour
1½ tsp. baking soda
½ tsp. salt
⅓ tsp. cinnamon

Butter Icing:
¼ c. butter
2 c. powdered sugar
2 Tbsp. cream
1 tsp. vanilla

Chill dough a little if too sticky. Put through cookie press in long strips on ungreased baking sheets. Bake at 350° until golden. Use cookie press to put frosting on cookie strip. Top with another cookie strip to form a sandwich. Press together and cut.

Maple Leaf Cutout Cookies

1 c. butter
2 c. brown sugar
4 eggs
6 Tbsp. cream or Rich's topping
2 Tbsp. maple flavoring
3 tsp. baking soda
½ tsp. salt
5¼ c. flour

Icing:
2 egg whites
4 tsp. milk
4 tsp. flour
4 tsp. vanilla
4 c. powdered sugar, divided
1½ c. shortening

Cream butter and sugar; add beaten eggs, cream and flavoring. Beat well. Add soda, salt and flour. Chill dough. Roll out onto floured surface until ¼" thick. Cut with a leaf shaped cookie cutter. Bake at 350° until golden. These cookies bake quickly. These are sandwich cookies. Beat together egg whites, milk, flour, vanilla and 2 c. powdered sugar. Add shortening and 2 c. powdered sugar. Blend until smooth.

Folded Date-Filled Cookies

1½ c. dates, cut fine
½ c. brown sugar
½ c. water

Dough:
½ c. butter
¾ c. brown sugar
1 egg
¾ c. oatmeal
1½ c. + 2 Tbsp. flour
½ tsp. soda
½ tsp. cream of tartar
¼ tsp. salt
½ tsp. vanilla

Combine dates, sugar and water. Boil for 10 minutes, stirring constantly. Cool date filling. Mix dough ingredients together. Chill for 1 hour. Roll out onto floured surface and cut with a 2½" round cutter. Spread 1 tsp. of date filling on half of each cookie and fold over. Do not overfill. Sealing edges is not necessary. Bake at 350° for at least 20 minutes. Do not underbake.

Debbie Cookies

½ c. butter
1½ c. brown sugar
1 tsp. vanilla
2 eggs
½ tsp. salt
1 tsp. cinnamon
¼ tsp. nutmeg
¾ tsp. baking soda
1½ c. oatmeal
1½ c. flour

Cream butter, sugar and vanilla. Beat eggs and add. Last stir in dry ingredients. Best if cookies are baked right away. Do not let set too long. Drop onto greased cookie sheets. Bake at 350° until golden. Do not overbake. Cookies have a better texture if mixed with a Bosch mixer. Mix filling and spread between 2 cookies. Makes approximately 1½ dozen doubles.

Filling:
2 egg whites, beaten
1½ tsp. vanilla
1 c. marshmallow topping
1½ c. powdered sugar
½ c. Crisco

[H I N T]

If you don't have baking powder, substitute ¼ tsp. soda plus 1 tsp. cream of tartar.

Brown Sugar Cookies

1 c. butter, softened
2 c. brown sugar
3 eggs
½ c. milk
1½ tsp. vanilla
3½ c. flour
2 tsp. baking powder
1 tsp. baking soda
⅛ tsp. salt

Icing:
¼ c. + 2 Tbsp. water
pinch of salt
½ tsp. vanilla
3 c. powdered sugar
½ c. + 2 Tbsp. shortening

Cream butter and sugar together. Add eggs and mix well. Add milk and vanilla. Last add dry ingredients. Bake at 400°. Mix water, salt, vanilla and powdered sugar. Add shortening. Beat well. Add as much powdered sugar as needed to make right consistency.

Strawberry Cream Cookies

1 c. butter, softened
1 c. white sugar
3 oz. cream cheese, softened
1 Tbsp. vanilla
1 egg
¼ tsp. salt
½ tsp. baking powder
2½ c. flour
strawberry jam

Cream butter, sugar and cream cheese. Add vanilla and egg. Mix well. Add dry ingredients. Chill dough. Shape into 1" balls and press on ungreased baking sheet. Using a floured thimble, press a dent in center of each ball. Fill with ½ tsp. jam. Bake at 350° for 10-12 minutes. Frost with white icing, leaving jam exposed.

Butter Balls

½ c. butter, softened
2½ Tbsp. powdered sugar
1 c. flour
½ tsp. vanilla
¼ c. finely chopped nuts

additional powdered sugar

Cream butter and powdered sugar; add flour gradually and mix. Add vanilla and nuts. Flour your hands and make rounded balls out of a tsp. of dough. Put on ungreased cookie sheets. Bake at 350° for 10 minutes or until just starting to brown. Place 1 c. powdered sugar on waxed paper or in a bowl. While hot, roll balls in powdered sugar, with hands well coated. Some will melt into cookies.

Soft Date Cookies

1 c. chopped dates
¼ c. white sugar
¼ c. + 2 Tbsp. water
1 c. brown sugar
½ c. shortening
2 sm. eggs
½ tsp. soda, dissolved in
    ½ Tbsp. water
½ tsp. salt
½ tsp. vanilla
1¾-2 c. flour

Boil dates, sugar and water over low heat for 5 minutes. Cool. Mix together remaining ingredients except flour. Then add date mixture. Add flour. Chill for 3-4 hours. Bake at 350°. Do not overbake. When cool, roll in powdered sugar.

Chocolate Sandwich Cookies

1 pkg. chocolate cake mix
½ c. vegetable oil
2 eggs

Filling:
3 oz. cream cheese, softened
2 Tbsp. butter, softened
1¼ c. powdered sugar
½ tsp. vanilla

Combine cake mix, oil and eggs. Mix well. Roll into 1" balls. Do not flatten. Bake at 350° for 8-10 minutes or until set. Combine cream cheese and butter; mix well. Add powdered sugar and vanilla. Beat until creamy. Spread on bottom of half of the cookies. Top with remaining cookies.

Double Chocolate Cookies

½ c. butter, softened
½ c. white sugar
½ c. brown sugar
1 egg
½ tsp. vanilla
1¼ c. old-fashioned oats
1 c. flour
½ tsp. baking soda
½ tsp. baking powder
¼ tsp. salt
1 c. chocolate chips
¾ c. chopped nuts
½ c. chocolate sprinkles

Cream butter and sugars. Add egg and vanilla; beat well. Place oats in blender or food processor. Cover and process until finely ground. Combine oats, flour, soda, baking powder and salt. Add gradually to creamed mixture. Stir in chocolate chips, nuts and sprinkles. Drop onto cookie sheets and flatten. Bake at 350°. You can use quick oats instead of processing the old-fashioned oats in blender.

Cookies

Special Oatmeal Cookies

½ c. butter, softened
½ c. peanut butter
½ c. white sugar
½ c. brown sugar
1 egg
½ tsp. vanilla
½ tsp. baking soda
1 tsp. cinnamon
⅛ tsp. ground nutmeg
1½ c. old-fashioned oats
½ c. flour
¾ c. chocolate chips

½ c. white chocolate
  confectionery coating
½ c. dark chocolate
  confectionery coating

Cream butter, peanut butter and sugars. Add egg, vanilla, soda, cinnamon and nutmeg. Gradually stir in oats and flour. Add chocolate chips. Drop onto cookie sheets and bake at 350° for 10-12 minutes or until lightly browned. Cool cookies. Drizzle with white chocolate coating in one direction, then with dark coating in opposite direction to form a crisscross pattern.

Chocolate Chip Toffee Cookies

¾ c. butter, softened
½ c. shortening
¾ c. brown sugar
¾ c. white sugar
2 eggs
⅔ c. instant vanilla pudding
2 tsp. vanilla
1 tsp. baking soda
3 c. flour
1½ c. chocolate chips
1 c. English toffee bits

Cream butter, shortening and sugars. Add eggs, instant pudding, vanilla and soda. Stir in flour; add chocolate chips and toffee bits. Drop onto baking sheets. Bake at 350° until lightly browned. Do not overbake.

Four-Chip Cookies

½ c. butter, softened
½ c. peanut butter
½ c. white sugar
⅓ c. brown sugar
1 egg
½ tsp. vanilla
1 c. flour
1 c. old-fashioned oats
1 tsp. baking soda
¼ tsp. salt
⅓ c. milk chocolate chips
⅓ c. vanilla chips
⅓ c. peanut butter chips
⅓ c. butterscotch chips

Cream butter, peanut butter and sugars. Add egg and vanilla; beat well. Combine flour, oats, soda and salt. Gradually add to creamed mixture. Stir in chips. Drop onto baking sheets. Bake at 350° for 10-12 minutes or until lightly browned.

Cream-Filled Toffee Cookies

½ c. butter, softened
½ c. brown sugar
¼ c. white sugar
1 egg
1 tsp. vanilla
1¼ c. flour
¼ tsp. baking soda
⅛ tsp. salt
½ c. English toffee bits

Cream Filling:
⅓ c. butter, softened
2 c. powdered sugar
½ tsp. vanilla
2-2½ Tbsp. half and half cream
   or milk

Cream butter and sugars; add egg and vanilla. Combine flour, baking soda and salt. Gradually add to creamed mixture. Stir in toffee bits. Dough will be stiff. Drop onto baking sheets. Bake at 350° for 10 minutes or until firm. Do not brown. Combine butter, powdered sugar, vanilla and enough cream to achieve spreading consistency. Spread on bottom of half of the cookies; top with remaining cookies.

Cookies

Sour Cream Cutouts

½ c. shortening
¾ c. white sugar
½ tsp. baking powder
1½ tsp. baking soda
¼ tsp. salt
2 eggs
½ c. sour cream
2 c. flour

Cream shortening, sugar, baking powder, soda and salt. Add eggs and sour cream. Mix well. Gradually add flour. Chill overnight. Roll thick and cut in desired shapes. Bake at 350° until bottom of cookies are lightly browned. Cool and ice with cream cheese frosting or Crisco frosting found in cake section of this book.

Mud Hen Bars

½ c. shortening
1 c. white sugar
1 egg
2 egg yolks
1½ c. flour
1 tsp. baking powder
¼ tsp. salt
1 c. nuts
½ c. chocolate chips
1 c. mini marshmallows
2 egg whites
1 c. brown sugar

Mix first 7 ingredients. Press into 9" x 13" pan. Sprinkle with nuts, chocolate chips and marshmallows. Beat egg whites until stiff, folding in brown sugar. Spread on top. Bake at 350° for 30-40 minutes.

Oh Henry Bars

¼ c. butter
½ c. shortening
½ c. brown sugar
3 c. oatmeal
¼ c. + 2 Tbsp. Karo
⅜ tsp. vanilla
1½ c. milk chocolate chips
½ c. peanut butter

Mix together butter, shortening, sugar, oatmeal, Karo and vanilla and put in greased 9" x 13" pan. Bake at 350° for 15 minutes. Do not overbake. Melt chocolate chips; stir in peanut butter. Spread over bars. Cool and cut.

S'more Bars

1 c. oatmeal
½ c. flour
½ c. brown sugar
¼ tsp. salt
¼ tsp. baking soda
½ c. butter, melted
2 c. mini marshmallows
½ c. milk chocolate chips

Combine oatmeal, flour, sugar, salt and soda. Stir in butter until crumbly. Press into a greased 11" x 7" baking dish. Bake at 350° for 10 minutes. Sprinkle with marshmallows and chocolate chips. Bake for 5-7 minutes longer until marshmallows begin to brown.

Fudgy Peanut Butter Bars

1 pkg. yellow cake mix
1 c. creamy peanut butter
1 egg
½ c. vegetable oil
1 can sweetened condensed milk
¾ c. chocolate chips
2 Tbsp. butter

Combine cake mix, peanut butter, egg and oil. Press ⅔ of mixture into a greased 9" x 13" pan. Bake at 350° for 10 minutes. Cool for 5 minutes. Heat the milk, chocolate chips and butter in a saucepan over low heat until chips are melted. Pour over crust. Sprinkle with remaining crumb mixture. Bake at 350° for 20-25 minutes, until golden brown. Cool and cut into bars.

[H I N T]

If a recipe calls for cold butter, shred it on a cheese grater. It's much faster than trying to cut it into workable pieces and it blends perfectly with the flour.

Cookies

Chocolate Streusel Bars

¾ c. flour
¾ c. powdered sugar
¼ c. cocoa
½ c. cold butter
4 oz. cream cheese, softened
½ c. sweetened condensed milk
1 sm. egg
1 tsp. vanilla
¼ c. chopped nuts

Preheat oven to 350°. Combine flour, sugar and cocoa. Cut in butter until crumbly. Reserve 1 c. crumb mixture. Press remainder firmly in a greased 8" square pan. Bake for 10-12 minutes. Beat cream cheese until fluffy. Stir in sweetened condensed milk until smooth. Add egg and vanilla. Pour over baked crust. Combine nuts with reserved crumbs. Sprinkle over cheese mixture. Bake for 15-20 minutes or until bubbly. Cool; cut into bars.

Double Chocolate Marshmallow Bars

1 pkg. fudge brownie mix or
    ½ pkg. chocolate cake mix
1 pkg. (10½ oz.) marshmallows
1½ c. milk chocolate chips
1 c. creamy peanut butter
1 Tbsp. butter
1½ c. crisp rice cereal

Prepare and bake brownies or cake mix according to package directions. When finished baking, sprinkle with marshmallows and put back in oven for 3 minutes. Combine chocolate chips, peanut butter and butter in medium saucepan over low heat. Stir constantly until chocolate chips are melted. Remove from heat and add crisp rice cereal; mix well. Spread mixture over marshmallows. Refrigerate until chilled; cut in bars.

Hershey Chocolate Mint Bars

Layer 1:
½ c. butter, softened
1 c. white sugar
4 eggs
1½ c. Hershey's syrup
1 c. flour

Layer 2:
½ c. butter, softened
2 c. powdered sugar
½ tsp. mint extract
1 Tbsp. hot water
4-5 drops green food coloring

Layer 3:
1 c. chocolate chips
6 Tbsp. butter

Beat Layer 1 ingredients until smooth. Put in 9" x 13" pan. Bake at 350° for 20 minutes; cool. Mix together Layer 2. Spread on cooled Layer 1; chill. Melt Layer 3 and spread on Layer 2.

Cream Cheese Brownies

½ pkg. chocolate cake mix
4 oz. cream cheese
1 sm. egg
¼ c. white sugar
¾ c. chocolate chips

Mix cake mix according to directions on package, using half the ingredients. Pour into greased 9" x 13" pan. Beat together cream cheese, egg and sugar. Drop onto cake batter with spoon; swirl with a knife. Sprinkle with chocolate chips. Bake at 350° for 30 minutes or until done.

Mom's Oh Henry Bars

½ c. butter
½ c. brown sugar
¼ c. white sugar
2 c. oatmeal
⅜ tsp. salt
½ tsp. vanilla
1 c. milk chocolate chips
¼ c. + 2 Tbsp. peanut butter

Mix butter, sugars, oatmeal, salt and vanilla and press into 9" x 13" greased pan. Bake for 15 minutes. Cool. Over low heat melt chocolate chips; add peanut butter. Stir constantly. Spread on bars. Cool; cut into bars.

Peanut Butter Fingers

½ c. butter
¼ c. + 2 Tbsp. peanut butter
½ c. white sugar
½ c. brown sugar
2 sm. eggs
½ tsp. baking soda
1 tsp. salt
½ tsp. vanilla
1 c. flour
1 c. oatmeal

1 c. chocolate chips

Frosting:
½ c. powdered sugar
¼ c. peanut butter
2-4 Tbsp. milk or
    to desired consistency

Cream butter, peanut butter and sugars. Add eggs, soda, salt and vanilla. Beat well; add flour and oatmeal. Spread into a 9" x 13" pan. Bake at 350° for 18-20 minutes. Sprinkle immediately with chocolate chips. Combine powdered sugar, peanut butter and milk. Drizzle frosting on top of warm bars and use a knife to swirl frosting and chocolate chips together.

Chocolate Caramel Bars

1 c. oatmeal
¾ c. flour
⅓ c. brown sugar
¼ tsp. soda
⅛ tsp. salt
⅓ c. butter, melted
½ Tbsp. water
½ c. chopped nuts
½ c. chocolate chips
½ c. caramel ice cream topping
2 Tbsp. flour

Preheat oven to 350°. Grease 8" square pan. Combine oatmeal, flour, sugar, soda, salt, melted butter and water. Reserve ½ c. crumbs. Press remainder in pan. Bake for 8-10 minutes or until light brown. Cool for 10 minutes. Top with nuts and chocolate chips. Mix caramel topping with 2 Tbsp. flour. Drizzle over chocolate chips. Sprinkle with reserved crumbs. Bake for 15-18 minutes.

Raisin Granola Bars

2 Tbsp. butter
2 Tbsp. vegetable oil
¾ lb. marshmallows
2 Tbsp. honey
2 Tbsp. peanut butter
2¼ c. Rice Krispies
½ c. graham cracker crumbs
2½ c. oatmeal
¾ c. raisins
½ c. coconut
½ c. chocolate chips

Melt butter and oil; stir in marshmallows until melted. Remove from heat and add honey and peanut butter. Mix dry ingredients. Make a well in center and pour in marshmallow mixture. Stir until combined. Press into a greased 9" x 13" pan. Cool and cut.

Granola Bars

½ c. butter
2 Tbsp. peanut butter
2 Tbsp. honey
2 Tbsp. vegetable oil
½ lb. marshmallows
1 pkg. graham crackers, crushed
2¼ c. Rice Krispies
1 c. oatmeal
½ c. coconut
½ c. chopped nuts
¼ c. chocolate chips
½ c. M&M's

In a large saucepan, melt butter; add peanut butter, honey, oil and marshmallows. Stir constantly until marshmallows are melted. In a large bowl, combine dry ingredients. Add marshmallow mixture and stir until coated. Pat into a greased 9" x 13" pan. Cool and cut into bars.

Fruit Squares

½ c. butter, softened
¾ c. + 2 Tbsp. sugar
2 eggs
½ tsp. vanilla
1½ c. flour
¾ tsp. baking powder
¼ tsp. salt
1 c. + 2 Tbsp. pie filling

Glaze:
¾ c. powdered sugar
¼ tsp. vanilla
warm water to desired consistency

Cream butter and sugar; add eggs and vanilla. Add dry ingredients. Spread ⅔ of batter in a greased 9" x 13" pan. Cover with pie filling. Dot with remaining batter. Bake at 350° for 20-30 minutes or until lightly browned and center is no longer doughy. Combine glaze ingredients. Drizzle over bars when cooled.

Delicious Lemon Bars

1 c. cold butter
2 c. flour
½ c. powdered sugar
pinch of salt
4 eggs, beaten
2 c. white sugar
6 Tbsp. lemon juice
4 Tbsp. flour

Mix butter, flour, powdered sugar and salt like pie dough. Pat into 9" x 13" pan. Bake at 350° for 15-20 minutes. Beat together eggs, white sugar, lemon juice and flour and pour over baked crust. Bake at 350° for approximately 25 minutes. Do not overbake. Sprinkle with powdered sugar.

Sour Cream Raisin Bars

½ c. butter, softened
½ c. packed brown sugar
¾ c. + 2 Tbsp. flour
1 c. oatmeal
½ tsp. baking powder
½ tsp. baking soda
pinch of salt

Filling:
2 egg yolks
1 Tbsp. clear jel or cornstarch
¾ c. raisins
1 c. sour cream
½ c. white sugar

In a large bowl, cream butter and brown sugar. Beat in flour, oatmeal, baking powder, soda and salt. Mixture will be crumbly. Set aside 1 c. crumbs. Pat remaining crumbs into a greased 9" x 13" pan. Bake at 350° for 15 minutes. Cool. Combine filling ingredients in a saucepan. Bring to a boil; cook, stirring constantly, for 5-8 minutes. Pour over crust. Sprinkle with reserved crumbs. Return to oven for 15 minutes.

Cookies

Napoleon Créme Bars

½ c. butter, softened
¼ c. cocoa
¼ c. white sugar
1 tsp. vanilla
1 egg, slightly beaten
2 c. graham cracker crumbs
1 c. coconut
½ c. butter
3¾ oz. instant vanilla pudding
3 Tbsp. milk
2 c. powdered sugar
1 c. chocolate chips
2 Tbsp. butter

Combine ½ c. butter, cocoa, white sugar and vanilla in a saucepan. Cook until butter melts. Stir in egg and cook until mixture thickens. Blend in crumbs and coconut. Press into a greased 9" x 9" pan. Cream ½ c. butter; stir in pudding mix, milk and powdered sugar. Beat until fluffy. Spread over cooled first layer. Chill until firm. Melt chocolate chips and 2 Tbsp. butter. Cool and spread onto pudding layer. Chill; cut into bars.

Frosted Pumpkin Bars

2 eggs, beaten
½ c. vegetable oil
1 c. white sugar
½ c. pumpkin
¼ tsp. salt
½ tsp. baking soda
½ tsp. baking powder
1 tsp. cinnamon
1 c. flour
½ c. chopped nuts

Frosting:
1½ oz. cream cheese
1¼ c. powdered sugar
3 Tbsp. butter, melted
½ tsp. milk
½ tsp. vanilla

Mix together and bake at 350° for 20 minutes in greased and floured 9" x 13" pan. Mix frosting ingredients and spread on bars while still warm.

Rich Apple Coffee Bars

1¼ c. flour
½ tsp. salt
1 tsp. sugar
1 tsp. baking powder
½ c. cold butter
1 egg yolk, beaten
2½ tsp. milk
apples
1½ Tbsp. flour
¾ c. white sugar
1 tsp. cinnamon
2 Tbsp. butter

Mix together flour, salt, sugar and baking powder; cut in butter. Stir in beaten egg yolk and milk. Pat into an ungreased 7" x 11" pan. Cover with apples cut into 16ths and laid in rows. Top with mixture of flour, white sugar, cinnamon and butter. Bake at 375° for 45-50 minutes.

Twinkies

½ pkg. white or yellow cake mix
¼ c. instant vanilla pudding
¼ c. + 2 Tbsp. vegetable oil
¼ c. + 2 Tbsp. water
2 eggs

Filling:
1 egg white, beaten
1½ c. powdered sugar
½ tsp. vanilla
½ c. shortening

Mix everything together and put into two well greased 9" x 13" pans. Bake at 350° for 15-20 minutes. When done put one pan on a wet towel and flip that one on the one with filling.

Pecan Pie Bars

⅔ c. white sugar
½ c. butter, softened
1 tsp. vanilla
1 egg
1½ c. flour
⅔ c. brown sugar
½ c. corn syrup
1 tsp. vanilla
3 eggs
1 c. coarsely chopped pecans

Mix white sugar, butter, 1 tsp. vanilla and 1 egg in a large bowl. Stir in flour; press dough in bottom and ½" up the sides of an ungreased 9" x 13" pan. Bake at 350° for 10-15 minutes or until edges are light brown. Beat brown sugar, corn syrup, 1 tsp. vanilla and 3 eggs. Stir in pecans with spoon. Pour over crust. Bake for 20 minutes or until set. Loosen edges from sides of pan while still warm. Cool and cut.

1-2-3 Coffee Bars

1 egg
½ c. vegetable oil
1⅓ c. brown sugar
½ c. warm coffee
½ tsp. salt
1½ c. flour
½ tsp. baking soda
½ tsp. vanilla
nuts
miniature chocolate chips

Mix first 8 ingredients in order given and put in greased 9" x 13" pan. Sprinkle with nuts and miniature chocolate chips. Bake at 350° until done. Cut in bars.

Chocolate Chip Cream Cheese Bars

2 c. chocolate chip cookie dough
⅔ c. cream cheese pastry filling

Press 1½ c. of cookie dough into greased 8" square baking dish. Spread cream cheese pastry filling over dough. Sprinkle remaining cookie dough on top. Bake at 350° for 20-25 minutes or until golden brown.

Many years ago, a household of two faced some unique challenges that we in a more modern era know nothing of. My great-grandparents, John and Anna, spent their days working hard at farming. Even though life wasn't always easy for them, it was not without its simple pleasures.

Every Saturday evening, during the summer, an Imperial ice cream truck would stop by and great-grandma and grandpa would buy themselves a half gallon of vanilla ice cream. Well, they had no refrigerator, much less a freezer, so what to do with all that ice cream? Eat it, of course! So, in one sitting, just the two of them, they would eat every last bite of that half gallon of ice cream! If they would have left some for the next morning, it would have been a milk shake. The morning after that, they would have had sour cream.

You would think eating all that ice cream over so many years would have had some adverse effect on their health, but apparently it didn't. Great-Grandma died at the age of 92, while Great-Grandpa lived to see the ripe old age of 105!

—*Sam*

Mini Apple Crisps

2 med. apples, peeled and sliced
½ c. flour
¼ c. brown sugar
2 Tbsp. butter
¼ c. oatmeal
¼ tsp. cinnamon

Place apple slices in a small greased baking dish. Combine flour and sugar. Cut in butter until crumbly. Add oatmeal and cinnamon. Sprinkle over apple slices. Bake uncovered at 350° for 30-35 minutes. Serve warm with ice cream.

Apple Crisp

½ Tbsp. flour
½ c. white sugar
⅛ tsp. salt
¼ tsp. cinnamon
2 c. sliced apples

Crumbs:
½ c. oatmeal
¼ c. brown sugar
½ c. all-purpose flour
⅛ tsp. baking soda
½ tsp. baking powder
6 Tbsp. butter, softened

Mix flour, sugar, salt and cinnamon with apples. Place in a greased 8" pie pan. Combine dry ingredients; cut in butter until crumbly. Place on top of apple mixture and bake at 350° for 30 minutes or until golden brown. Serve warm with ice cream.

Baked Apples

2 apples, peeled and sliced
¾ c. brown sugar
2 Tbsp. flour
¾ c. water
¼ tsp. cinnamon
1 Tbsp. butter

Place apples in baking dish. Mix brown sugar and flour; add water and cinnamon. Pour over apples; dot with butter. Bake at 350° until apples are tender. Serve with whipped cream.

Desserts

Rhubarb Cake Dessert

½ c. butter, softened
1 Tbsp. white sugar
1 c. flour
2½ c. rhubarb, chopped
2 Tbsp. flour
3 egg yolks
½ c. cream
¾ c. white sugar
⅛ tsp. salt

Meringue:
3 egg whites, beaten
½ c. white sugar
1 Tbsp. vanilla
pinch of salt

Crumble together butter, sugar and flour and press into greased 8" x 8" pan. Mix remaining ingredients and pour on top of crumb mixture. Bake at 350° for 30-35 minutes. Beat egg whites until stiff. Gradually beat in sugar; add vanilla and salt. Put on top of baked filling and bake until golden. Delicious served warm.

Peach Cobbler

3 c. fresh, sliced peaches
1 c. white sugar
1½ c. flour
3 tsp. baking powder
½ tsp. salt
⅓ c. shortening
¼ c. milk
1 egg
2 Tbsp. white sugar

Put peaches and 1 c. sugar in greased 7" x 11" baking dish. Warm peaches and sugar in oven. Mix flour, baking powder, salt, shortening, milk and egg together. Drop by spoonful over the top of peaches. Sprinkle with 2 Tbsp. white sugar. Bake at 400° for 30 minutes. Delicious served warm and eaten with milk.

[HINT]

Combine broken chocolate or angel food cake, whipped cream, chopped nuts, marshmallows and chopped candied fruits. Scoop into sherbet glasses and chill for 3 hours.

Blueberry Fruit Salad

½ c. pineapple chunks, undrained
½ c. sliced peaches, undrained
1 c. fresh or frozen blueberries
1 banana, sliced
½ c. sliced, fresh strawberries
½ c. halved green grapes
¼ c. instant vanilla pudding
1½ Tbsp. powdered orange drink mix

Reserve the juice from pineapples and peaches; set aside. Combine all the fruit in a bowl. Combine fruit juices with pudding and drink mix. Mix well. Pour over fruit and toss to coat. Refrigerate until serving.

Apricot Berry Shortcake

1 c. fresh raspberries
    or blackberries
1 Tbsp. white sugar
¼ c. apricot jam
1 tsp. butter
dash of salt
2 individual round sponge cakes
whipped cream

In a bowl combine the berries and sugar. Refrigerate for 1 hour. In a saucepan, heat jam, butter and salt on low until butter is melted. Warm the sponge cakes in the oven for 7 minutes. Place on serving plates. Top with berries and drizzle with apricot sauce. Garnish with dollop of whipped cream.

Blueberry Cream Dessert

¾ c. graham cracker crumbs
¼ c. butter, melted
2 Tbsp. white sugar
3 oz. cream cheese, softened
¼ c. white sugar
1 egg
½ tsp. vanilla
¼ tsp. cinnamon
½ c. blueberry pie filling
1½ c. Cool Whip

Combine crackers, butter and 2 Tbsp. white sugar. Press into a greased 8" square baking dish. Beat cream cheese and ¼ c. white sugar until smooth; add egg and vanilla. Pour over crust. Bake at 350° for 12-15 minutes or until set. Sprinkle with cinnamon. Cool completely. Spread with pie filling and Cool Whip. Refrigerate until serving.

White Chocolate Parfaits

½ c. whipping cream
2 Tbsp. sugar
1 tsp. cornstarch
1 egg yolk
2 sq. white baking chocolate
½ tsp. vanilla
1½ c. whipped topping
¾ c. fresh red raspberries
¾ c. fresh blueberries

In a saucepan, heat the cream just to a boil. In a bowl, combine sugar and cornstarch. Add egg yolk. Stir small amount of hot cream into yolk mixture; return all to pan. Cook and stir for 2 minutes or until mixture reaches 160° and is thickened. Stir in chocolate until melted; add vanilla. Cool to room temperature. Fold in whipped topping. Place ¼ c. each in 2 parfait glasses. Combine berries; place ¼ c. on pudding. Repeat layers of pudding and berries twice. Chill for at least 1 hour.

Blueberry Sherbet

1 c. sour cream
¾ c. white sugar
1 Tbsp. lemon juice
½ tsp. vanilla
3 c. fresh or frozen blueberries
Cool Whip, optional

In a blender, combine all ingredients except Cool Whip. Cover and process until smooth. Press through sieve. Discard blueberry skins and seeds. Freeze for 8 hours or overnight. Remove from freezer 30 minutes before serving. Top with Cool Whip if desired. This can also be made with raspberries or strawberries.

[H I N T]

For evenly sliced kiwi fruit, peel and slice using an egg slicer.

Raspberry Cheesecake Trifle

3 oz. cream cheese, softened
1 Tbsp. powdered sugar
1 c. Cool Whip
2 c. cubed white cake
1 c. fresh raspberries
2 Tbsp. grated chocolate

Beat cream cheese and powdered sugar until smooth. Fold in Cool Whip. In individual bowls, layer half the cake cubes, ¼ c. raspberries, half the cream cheese mixture and half the chocolate. Repeat layers. Reserve a few raspberries for garnish. Refrigerate 4 hours or overnight.

Layered Blueberry Delight

8 whole graham crackers
3½ oz. instant vanilla pudding
½ c. Cool Whip
1½ c. blueberry pie filling

Line a small dish with graham crackers. Prepare pudding mix according to package directions. Let set for 5 minutes. Fold in Cool Whip. Spread half of pudding mixture over crackers. Top with another layer of crackers. Top with remaining pudding and more crackers. Spread pie filling on top layer of crackers; chill.

Strawberry Pretzel Dessert

1 c. finely crushed pretzels
⅓ c. butter, melted
1½ Tbsp. white sugar
¼ c. powdered sugar
4 oz. cream cheese, softened
1½ c. Cool Whip
1 c. mini marshmallows
3 oz. strawberry Jell-O
1¼ c. boiling water
1 c. fresh or frozen
     sliced strawberries

Mix pretzels, butter and sugar. Press into 8" square pan. Bake at 350° for 15 minutes. Cool. Cream powdered sugar and cream cheese; fold in Cool Whip. Add marshmallows; spread on cooled crust. Dissolve Jell-O in boiling water. Chill until slightly thickened. Stir in the strawberries. Spread over cream cheese layer. Chill.

Mini Cheesecakes

½ c. white sugar
8 oz. cream cheese, softened
1 egg
1½ tsp. lemon juice
½ tsp. vanilla
vanilla wafer cookies

Cream sugar and cream cheese until fluffy; beat in egg, lemon juice and vanilla. Put a vanilla wafer on the bottom of paper-lined muffin pans. Fill liners ⅔ full with cream cheese mixture. Bake at 375° for 15 minutes. Chill. Top with your choice of fruit pie filling before serving.

Tropical Fruit Dessert

¼ c. white sugar
2 Tbsp. clear jel
¼ tsp. tropical punch Kool-Aid
1 c. cold water
½ c. pineapple tidbits, drained
2 bananas, sliced
½ c. red seedless grapes

In a saucepan, combine dry ingredients. Stir in cold water. Bring to a boil over medium heat, stirring constantly until clear. Remove from heat and cool. Chill in refrigerator, then add fruit.

Cheesecake

½ pkg. white cake mix
8 oz. cream cheese, softened
1¾ c. powdered sugar
1 c. whipping cream, whipped
pie filling of your choice

Mix cake mix according to package directions, using half the ingredients. Bake in greased 8" square pan until done; cool. Beat cream cheese and powdered sugar until fluffy. Fold in whipped cream. Spread on cake. Chill for 4 hours. Top with pie filling.

[H I N T]

If you freeze berries or rhubarb for future baking projects, pre-measure the amounts called for in your favorite recipes. This allows you to quickly make your dessert later without messy measuring of frozen ingredients.

Luscious Raspberry Angel Squares

¼ angel food cake
¼ c. red raspberry Jell-O
½ c. boiling water
3 oz. cream cheese, softened
¼ c. white sugar
1 tsp. lemon juice
1½ c. Cool Whip, divided
fresh raspberries
mint leaves

Cut the angel food cake in 1" cubes. Place cubes in a greased 8" square dish. In a bowl, dissolve Jell-O in boiling water. Refrigerate until mixture just begins to thicken. Beat cream cheese, sugar and lemon juice until smooth. Add gelatin mixture; beat until combined. Fold in ¾ c. Cool Whip. Spread over cake cubes, covering completely. Refrigerate for 1½-2 hours or until firm. Top with remaining Cool Whip. Cut into squares. Garnish with fresh raspberries and mint leaves.

Lemon Pudding Dessert

½ c. cold butter
1 c. all-purpose flour
4 oz. cream cheese
½ c. powdered sugar
1½ c. whipped topping
1½ c. cold milk
1 pkg. instant lemon pudding

Cut butter into flour until crumbly. Press into an ungreased 8" square baking dish. Bake at 350° for 15-18 minutes or until set. Cool on wire rack. Beat cream cheese and sugar until smooth. Fold in ½ c. whipped topping. Spread over crust. Beat milk and pudding mix on low speed for 2 minutes. Carefully spread over cream cheese layer; top with remaining whipped topping. Refrigerate at least 1 hour before serving.

Fruit Hash

1 orange
1 banana
1 c. dates
1 c. red seedless grapes
⅓ c. walnuts or pecans
milk

Cut up orange, banana and dates. Add to grapes. Add nuts. Divide into 2 small fruit bowls and add milk.

Frozen Cheesecake

Crust:
1 pkg. graham crackers, crushed
6 Tbsp. butter, melted
3 Tbsp. brown sugar

Filling:
8 oz. cream cheese
½ c. white sugar
½ tsp. vanilla
2 eggs, well beaten
½ c. Rich's topping, whipped

Mix crust ingredients and press into bottom of 8" square pan. Mix together rest of ingredients, pour over cracker crust and freeze. Remove from freezer 15-30 minutes before serving. Serve with any kind of pie filling. This will keep awhile in freezer.

[H I N T]

For peppermint flavored ice cream, crush hard peppermint candies or candy canes and mix with softened vanilla ice cream.

Fancy Frozen Fruit Cups

½ c. water
¼ c. white sugar
¼ c. orange juice concentrate
¼ c. lemonade concentrate
½ c. pineapple tidbits, drained
½ c. sliced bananas
½ c. watermelon chunks
½ c. green grapes
½ c. quartered strawberries
½ c. cubed peaches
½ c. quartered and sliced kiwis

Bring water and sugar to a boil, stirring constantly. Remove from heat; stir in orange juice and lemonade concentrates. Combine pineapples, bananas, watermelon, grapes, strawberries and peaches. Add juice mixture and mix well. Place about 1 c. of fruit mixture in individual clear plastic cups. Top each with kiwi pieces. Cover and freeze until firm. May be frozen up to 1 month. Remove from freezer about 1¾ hours before serving. Store in freezer container with lid.

Yogurt

2 qt. milk
1 Tbsp. unflavored gelatin
¼ c. cold water
¼ c. plain yogurt
½ c. white sugar
pie filling of your choice

Heat milk to 180°. Cool to 130°. Dissolve gelatin in cold water. Add to milk. Beat in yogurt and sugar. Set in a warm place overnight. Refrigerate a few hours, then skim off the skin on top before adding pie filling. Beat well; refrigerate.

Triple Orange Salad

1 sm. box orange Jell-O
1 sm. box instant vanilla pudding
1 sm. box vanilla tapioca pudding
2½ c. water
1 can mandarin oranges, drained
2 c. Cool Whip

Mix Jell-O, puddings and water in a saucepan. Stir and bring to a full boil. Remove from heat and cool. Add oranges and Cool Whip. Mix well and garnish with more whip and orange slices.

Orange Sherbet Dessert

3 oz. orange Jell-O
1 c. boiling water
1 c. orange sherbet
½ c. mandarin oranges
1 c. crushed pineapples
clear jel
1-1½ c. Cool Whip

Dissolve Jell-O in boiling water; stir in sherbet. Add oranges and crushed pineapples, reserving pineapple juice. Chill Jell-O mixture until set. Bring pineapple juice to a boil and thicken with clear jel. Cool; add Cool Whip. Spread on top of Jell-O.

Candy Bar Ice Cream

2½ c. vanilla ice cream, softened
1 Tbsp. fudge ice cream topping
2 (2 oz.) Snickers candy bars, chopped

In a blender combine ice cream and fudge topping; process until smooth. Remove from blender and stir in candy bars. Freeze for 4 hours or until firm. May be frozen for up to 2 months.

Almond Delight

⅓ c. chocolate chips
¼ c. peanut butter, softened
1½ c. Almond Delight cereal
1 qt. vanilla ice cream

Melt chocolate chips and peanut butter over low heat. Stir in cereal and cool. Reserve ½ c. coated cereal. Mix the rest with ice cream. Pour into small pan and sprinkle with remaining cereal. Freeze.

[H I N T]

Keep fresh strawberries in the refrigerator by placing them in a Tupperware and covering with a paper towel. Put lid on. The paper towel absorbs the moisture and they will stay fresh longer.

Sherbet Surprise

3 c. crushed Rice Krispies
½ c. butter, melted
½ c. brown sugar
1½ c. Cool Whip
1½ Tbsp. white sugar
½ tsp. vanilla
1 c. pineapple sherbet
1 c. lime sherbet
1 c. raspberry sherbet

Combine Rice Krispies, butter and brown sugar. Set aside ½ c. for topping. Press remaining mixture in an 8" square dish. Mix Cool Whip, sugar and vanilla. Spread over crust. Arrange small scoops of sherbet over the top. Sprinkle with reserved crumbs. Cover and freeze until firm.

Frozen Ice Cream Pudding

1 lb. sandwich créme cookies
¼ c. butter, softened
1 c. powdered sugar
2 egg yolks, well beaten
1 sq. baking chocolate, melted
½ tsp. vanilla
¼ c. chopped walnuts
2 egg whites, stiffly beaten
1 qt. vanilla ice cream

Crush cookies and spread half over bottom of 8" square pan. Cream butter and sugar. Add egg yolks, melted chocolate, vanilla and nuts. Beat until fluffy. Fold in egg whites. Spread over crumbs; add ice cream and spread evenly. Sprinkle rest of cookies over top. Cover and freeze.

Chocolate Éclair Dessert

1¼ c. milk
½ c. instant vanilla pudding
¾ c. Cool Whip
graham crackers

Topping:
¼ c. chocolate chips
¾ Tbsp. butter
¾ Tbsp. milk
½ Tbsp. corn syrup
¾ tsp. vanilla
⅓ c. powdered sugar

Mix milk and pudding mix; let stand until set. Fold in Cool Whip. Line 1-qt. dish with graham crackers. Pour half the pudding over crackers. Top with another layer crackers. Add remaining pudding. Cover with another layer crackers. Melt chocolate chips and butter; add remaining topping ingredients, adding powdered sugar last. Stir well and spread over crackers. Refrigerate for at least 2 hours before serving.

Chocolate Cream Cheese Pudding

6 oz. milk chocolate chips
8 oz. cream cheese, softened
¾ c. brown sugar, divided
½ tsp. salt
1 tsp. vanilla
2 egg whites
2 c. heavy cream, whipped
8" graham cracker crust

Melt chocolate chips over hot but not boiling water. Cool 10 minutes. Blend in cream cheese, ½ c. sugar, salt and vanilla. Beat egg whites until very stiff. Fold chocolate chip mixture into beaten egg whites. Fold in whipped cream. Pour into crust and chill overnight.

[H I N T]

Sundae Idea—Drizzle chocolate sauce over a scoop of strawberry ice cream and top with sliced berries and kiwi.

Chocolate Cookie Cake

22 mini chocolate chip cookies
2 Tbsp. butter, melted
¾ c. fudge topping, divided
2 c. vanilla ice cream, softened
2 c. chocolate ice cream, softened

Crush 12 cookies; set remaining cookies aside. Combine cookie crumbs and butter. Press into bottom of a greased 7" springform pan. Freeze for 15 minutes. Heat ¼ c. fudge topping until pourable; spread over crust. Arrange reserved cookies around the edge of pan. Freeze for 15 minutes. Spread vanilla ice cream over fudge topping. Freeze for 30 minutes. Spread with chocolate ice cream. Cover and freeze until firm. May be frozen for up to 2 months. Remove from freezer for 10 minutes before serving. Remove sides of pan. Drizzle with remaining fudge topping.

Fudge Sundae Dessert

¼ c. Karo
2 Tbsp. brown sugar
3 Tbsp. butter
2½ c. Rice Krispies
¼ c. peanut butter
¼ c. fudge sauce
3 Tbsp. Karo
1 qt. ice cream, softened

Mix ¼ c. Karo, brown sugar and butter; cook over low heat until it boils. Remove from heat and add Rice Krispies until coated. Press into 8" square pan. Stir in peanut butter, fudge sauce and 3 Tbsp. Karo. Pour half of mixture on the Rice Krispies and freeze until firm. Top with ice cream and drizzle with remaining fudge mixture on top. Freeze.

Snicker Bar Dessert

1 qt. vanilla ice cream, softened
⅓ c. instant vanilla pudding
⅓ c. instant chocolate pudding
3 c. Cool Whip
½ c. crunchy peanut butter

Mix all ingredients and freeze.

Chocolate Malt Shoppe Pie

1½ c. chocolate cookie crumbs
¼ c. butter, melted
1 pt. vanilla ice cream, softened
½ c. crushed malted milk balls
2 Tbsp. milk, divided
3 Tbsp. instant malted
   milk powder
3 Tbsp. marshmallow créme
1 c. whipping cream, whipped

Combine crumbs and butter. Press into 9" pie pan. Freeze while preparing filling. Blend ice cream, crushed malted milk balls and 1 Tbsp. milk. Spoon onto crust; freeze for 1 hour. Blend malted milk powder, marshmallow créme and 1 Tbsp. milk. Fold in whipped cream. Spread over ice cream layer. Freeze for several hours or overnight. Garnish with Cool Whip and malted milk balls.

Rice Krispie Pie

1 Tbsp. butter, melted
½ c. marshmallow créme
2 c. Rice Krispies
vanilla ice cream
hot fudge sauce or
   fruit filling

Melt butter and marshmallow créme. Stir until smooth. Add cereal. Press into sides and bottom of greased 8" pie plate. Freeze for 20 minutes. Fill with vanilla ice cream. Freeze. Serve with hot fudge sauce or fruit filling.

Chocolate Cream Puffs

¼ c. water
2 Tbsp. butter
pinch of salt
¼ c. all-purpose flour
¾ Tbsp. cocoa
1 egg
4 oz. cream cheese, softened
¼ c. white sugar
½ c. whipping cream, whipped
¾ c. coarsely chopped fresh
   strawberries

In a saucepan over medium heat bring water, butter and salt to a boil. Add flour and cocoa all at once. Stir until a smooth ball forms. Remove from heat. Let set 5 minutes. Add the egg, beating well. Beat until smooth and shiny. Drop by heaping tablespoons 3" apart on a greased baking sheet. Bake at 400° for 30-35 minutes, until set and browned. Immediately split puffs open. Remove and discard dough from inside; cool completely. Beat cream cheese and sugar until fluffy; fold in whipped cream and strawberries. Fill bottom halves of puffs; replace tops. Serve immediately.

Tapioca Pudding

4 c. boiling water
½ c. + 1 Tbsp. baby pearl tapioca
⅓ c. strawberry Jell-O, or
   flavor of your choice
⅔ c. white sugar
pinch of salt
1 pt. Rich's topping, whipped
2 c. sweetened, chopped
   strawberries, optional

Combine water and baby pearl tapioca and cook for 10 minutes. Turn off heat and let set for 15 minutes or until tapioca is clear. Reheat and add Jell-O, sugar and salt. When cooled add Rich's topping and strawberries.

Snicker Tapioca Dessert

2½ c. water
¾ c. pearl tapioca
pinch of salt
¾ c. white sugar
1½ c. Cool Whip
¼ tsp. maple flavoring
½ tsp. vanilla
1 c. vanilla ice cream
3 Snickers candy bars, chopped

Pour tapioca into boiling water with salt and cook on low heat for 10 minutes. Cover and remove from heat. Let set for 20 minutes; add sugar and set aside overnight. When cold, add Cool Whip, maple flavoring, vanilla, ice cream and candy bars. Garnish with candy bars.

Upside-Down Date Pudding

1 c. dates, chopped
1 c. boiling water
½ c. white sugar
½ c. brown sugar
1 egg
2 Tbsp. butter, melted
1 tsp. salt
½ tsp. baking powder
1 tsp. baking soda
1½ c. flour
1 c. chopped nuts

Sauce:
1½ c. brown sugar
1½ c. boiling water
1 Tbsp. butter

Mix dates with boiling water; let cool. Blend sugars, egg and butter. Add dry ingredients to sugar mixture. Stir in nuts and cooled date mixture. Pour into a greased 7" x 11" baking dish; top with sauce. Bake at 350° for 45 minutes. When cold, cut into squares and invert onto serving plate. Dollop with Cool Whip.

[H I N T]

Sundae Idea—Place a scoop of chocolate or chocolate mint ice cream on a brownie. Pour on the hot fudge sauce. Add a spoonful of whipped cream, sprinkle with peanuts and accent with a maraschino cherry or a chocolate kiss.

Date Pudding

1 c. boiling water
1 c. chopped dates
1 tsp. baking soda
1 Tbsp. butter
1 c. white sugar
1 egg, beaten
1 c. all-purpose flour
½ c. chopped nuts

Caramel Sauce:
2 Tbsp. butter
1 c. brown sugar
1½ c. cold water, divided
2½ Tbsp. clear jel
¾ tsp. vanilla
½ tsp. maple flavoring

Pour boiling water over dates, soda and butter. Cool. Mix sugar, egg, flour and nuts. Add this to cooled date mixture. Pour into a greased 9" square pan. Bake at 350° for 20-25 minutes or until toothpick comes out clean. Bring butter, brown sugar and 1 c. cold water to a boil. Mix ½ c. water and clear jel. Add to sugar mixture. Cook until clear; remove from heat and add vanilla and maple flavoring. Cool the sauce. To serve, cut the date cake into 1" cubes and layer in a serving bowl with caramel sauce and whipped topping.

Graham Cracker Pudding

2 egg yolks
2 c. milk
2 heaping Tbsp. clear jel
½ c. white sugar
¼ tsp. salt
1 tsp. vanilla
1 c. Cool Whip
graham cracker crumbs
sliced bananas
additional Cool Whip

Whisk egg yolks into milk and bring to a boil. Mix clear jel, sugar and salt. Gradually stir into milk. Cook until thick; add vanilla. Chill. Add Cool Whip. To serve, layer graham cracker crumbs, custard and sliced bananas. Put Cool Whip on the top layer. Sprinkle with graham cracker crumbs.

Butterscotch Heath Bar Pudding

1 c. Ritz cracker crumbs
¼ c. butter, melted
¼ c. instant vanilla pudding
¼ c. instant butterscotch pudding
1 c. milk
1 qt. vanilla ice cream
1 c. Cool Whip
1 Heath bar, crushed

Mix cracker crumbs and butter; press into an 8" square pan. Mix puddings with milk; gradually stir in ice cream. Spread on top of crackers. Top with Cool Whip. Sprinkle Heath bar on top. Chill.

Chocolate Chip Torte

½ c. butter, softened
½ c. brown sugar
¼ c. white sugar
1 egg
½ tsp. vanilla
1¼ c. flour
½ tsp. salt
½ tsp. baking soda
½ c. milk chocolate chips
¼ c. instant vanilla pudding
1 c. milk
1½ c. Cool Whip

Cream butter and sugars; add egg and vanilla. Beat until light and fluffy. Add flour, salt and soda. Add chocolate chips. Spread into a greased 8" square pan. Bake at 350° for 12-15 minutes or until toothpick comes out clean. Don't overbake. Cool. Beat instant pudding and milk. Let it thicken, then spread on crust. Top with Cool Whip. Garnish with chocolate chips. Serve immediately.

Oreo Pudding Dessert

3 c. crushed Oreo cookies
¼ c. butter, melted
¼ c. white sugar
3 oz. cream cheese
½ c. powdered sugar
⅔ c. instant vanilla pudding
1½ c. milk
½ c. Cool Whip

Mix together cookies, butter and sugar. Press 2 c. into an 8" square pan. Cream together cream cheese and powdered sugar. Beat instant pudding and milk; let set until thickened. Add to cream cheese mixture. Fold in Cool Whip. Pour over the Oreo cookies in pan. Sprinkle with remaining 1 c. Oreo cookies. Chill until serving.

Cream Cheese Dessert

½ pkg. chocolate cake mix
4 oz. cream cheese, softened
¼ c. white sugar
1 egg yolk
¼ c. chocolate chips

Topping:
1 c. milk
½ c. instant vanilla pudding
8 oz. Cool Whip

Prepare cake mix according to package directions, using half the ingredients. Pour into greased 9" square pan. Beat cream cheese and sugar until creamy; add egg yolk and chips. Drop by tsp. over cake batter and swirl with a knife. Bake at 350° for 15-20 minutes or until toothpick comes out clean. Cool. Beat milk and pudding. Let set until thickened. Fold in Cool Whip. Spoon over the cake. Top with peach pie filling or fruit filling of your choice.

Swiss Meringue Shells

1 egg white
1¹⁄₁₆ tsp. cream of tartar
¼ c. white sugar
⅛ tsp. vanilla
fresh berries of your choice,
    blueberries, raspberries, etc.

Beat egg white and cream of tartar until foamy. Gradually beat in sugar, 1 Tbsp. at a time, until stiff and glossy. Beat in vanilla. Cover a baking sheet with greased foil or parchment paper. Spoon meringue into 2 mounds on the paper. Using the back of a spoon, shape into 3" cups. Bake at 250° for 1¼ hours. Cool on wire rack. Fill shells with berries. Garnish with Cool Whip or vanilla ice cream.

Baked Custard

1 egg
1 c. milk
3 Tbsp. white sugar
¾ tsp. vanilla
⅛ tsp. salt
⅛ tsp. ground nutmeg

Lightly beat egg; add milk, sugar, vanilla and salt. Pour into 2 ungreased custard cups. Sprinkle with nutmeg. Set in pan containing ½-1" hot water. Bake at 350° for 35 minutes or until set.

Desserts

Lizzie Pudding

1 c. graham cracker crumbs
2 tsp. powdered sugar
¼ tsp. unflavored gelatin
¼ c. butter, melted

Filling:
¾ c. Rich's topping
¼ c. + 2 Tbsp. powdered sugar
6 oz. cream cheese, softened
¾ tsp. vanilla

pie filling of your choice

Mix graham cracker crumbs, powdered sugar, unflavored gelatin and butter together. Press into a 9" square pan. Whip Rich's topping and beat together with powdered sugar, cream cheese and vanilla. Refrigerate for a few hours, then top with pie filling.

Fruit Pizza

¼ c. butter, softened
1 c. brown sugar
1 egg
1 c. flour
1 tsp. baking powder
¼ tsp. salt
1 tsp. vanilla

Filling:
4 oz. cream cheese, softened
2 Tbsp. white sugar
¾ c. Cool Whip

Pineapple Glaze:
1 c. pineapple juice
¼ c. white sugar
¾ Tbsp. clear jel

fresh fruit

Combine butter and sugar; add egg. Stir well. Stir in flour, baking powder, salt and vanilla. Spread in greased 9" square pan. Bake at 350° for 10-12 minutes. Cool. Mix filling and spread over crust. Bring pineapple juice, sugar and clear jel to a boil. Cook until clear. Cool. Arrange fresh fruit over cream cheese layer. Spoon pineapple glaze over fruit.

Drumstick Dessert

¾ c. + 2 Tbsp. crushed
 vanilla wafers
¼ c. crushed peanuts
1 Tbsp. peanut butter

Filling:
2 eggs
¼ c. white sugar
1 tsp. vanilla
4 oz. cream cheese, softened
¼ c. peanut butter
8 oz. Cool Whip
¼ c. + 2 Tbsp. fudge syrup

Mix wafers, peanuts and peanut butter, reserving ½ c. Put the rest into an 8" square greased pan with lid. Beat eggs, white sugar, vanilla, cream cheese and peanut butter with mixer until smooth, then fold in Cool Whip. Pour over crust. Dab fudge syrup onto filling. Run fork through chocolate. Sprinkle with reserved crust mix. Freeze for several hours or overnight before serving.

Ice Cream Sandwich Pudding

chocolate ice cream wafers
vanilla ice cream
Cool Whip
chocolate syrup

In a small pan put a layer of chocolate ice cream wafers. On top of that put a layer of vanilla ice cream, then another layer of wafers. If pan is very deep, you can repeat layers. Top with some Cool Whip. Drizzle with chocolate syrup if desired. Freeze several hours or overnight before serving.

Oreo Ice Cream Dessert

crushed Oreo cookies
butter, melted
vanilla ice cream, softened
Cool Whip
hot fudge sauce

Put crushed cookies, mixed with melted butter, in a small pan, reserving some for top. Spread ice cream over cookies. Top with Cool Whip, hot fudge sauce and reserved cookie crumbs. Freeze.

Desserts

[H I N T]

Sundae Idea—Like s'mores? Try topping vanilla ice cream with chocolate sauce, mini marshmallows, whipped cream and graham cracker crumbs.

Index

Index

Breads, Biscuits and Muffins

Main Dishes

Cakes and Frostings

Cookies

Table for Two

Desserts

VOLUME I

Cooking with the Horse & Buggy People

A Collection of Over 600 Favorite Recipes from the Heart of Holmes County

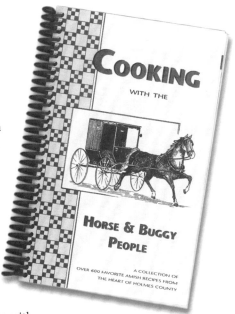

From mouth watering Amish style main dishes to kitchen dream desserts, this one has it all. Over 600 made-from-scratch recipes that please the appetite and are easy on the food budget. You'll get a whole section on canning and food preparation. The Amish, long known for their originality in the kitchen, share their favorites with you. If you desire originality, if you respect authenticity, if the Amish style cooking satisfies your taste palate—**Cooking With The Horse & Buggy People** is for you.

Contains 14 Complete Sections:

Breads, Cakes, Cookies, Desserts, Pies, Salads, Main Dishes, Soups, Cereal, Candy, Miscellaneous, Drinks, Canning, Home Remedies & Preparing Wild Game, Index.

· 5$^{1}/_{2}$" x 8$^{1}/_{2}$" · 275 pp · Spiral Bound · Laminated Cover · Convenient Thumb Index

Cooking with the Horse & Buggy People ... Item #164 ... $**11.99**

TO ORDER COOKBOOKS

Check your local bookstore or call **1-800-852-4482.**

VOLUME II

Cooking with the
Horse & Buggy People

Sharing a Second Serving of Favorites
from 207 Amish Women of Holmes County, Ohio

Henry and Amanda Mast, authors and compilers of *Cooking with the Horse and Buggy People Volume II* (as well as Volume I), live close to Charm, Ohio. Their home place is in the heart of the world's largest Amish community. The Masts and their friends worked countless hours in the kitchen to perfect the 600 recipes they chose to share with you.

Good food. Laughter. Compliments. Memories. That's what this new volume of *Cooking with the Horse and Buggy People* is about.

· 5¹/₂" x 8¹/₂" · 320 pp · Spiral Bound · Extra-Heavy Laminated Cover

Cooking with the Horse & Buggy People … Item #628 … **$11.99**

Give Us This Day Our Daily Bread

All the favorites of the Belle Center Amish Community. Over 600 of today's family favorites and even some from Grandma's kitchen. All the usual sections are here. But what makes this one special is the appetizers, large quantity recipes (for weddings, reunions, and other special occasions) and the children's recipe section. The tips, hints, and quotes section is filled with everyday kitchen secrets.

· 5¹/₂" x 8¹/₂" · 263 pp · Spiral bound · Indexed

Give Us This Day Our Daily Bread … Item #733 … **$11.99**

AUTHENTIC AMISH COOKING

The Wooden Spoon Cookbook

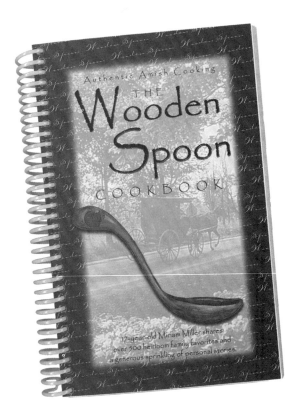

Meet 17-year-old Miriam Miller in the *Wooden Spoon Cookbook*. In addition to sharing her own, her mother's, and her grandmother's favorite recipes, Miriam shares childhood memories, stories, and personal details of her life as a young Amish girl.

· 5¹/₂" x 8¹/₂" · 194 pp · Spiral bound · Laminated cover · Double indexed

The Wooden Spoon Cookbook … Item #415 … **$10.99**

Wedding Sampler Cookbook

Here's a chance to experience the wedding of Amish bride Miriam Miller. Relax and sip the drink served at her bridal table. Enjoy the hearty main dishes and mouthwatering desserts served to her 500 guests. Miriam shares glimpses into the wedding as she talks about the preparation and serving of food on her special day. The icing on the cake with this cookbook is that Aden's (Miriam's husband) family have opened their recipe boxes and shared over 350 of their family favorites!

· 5¹/₂" x 8¹/₂" · Spiral bound · Laminated cover · Indexed

Wooden Spoon Wedding Sampler Cookbook … Item #005 … $**10.99**

Amish Quilting Cookbook

Sara Yoder

Fix up your favorite meal and enjoy the beauty of quilts at the same time with the new Quilting Cookbook. Its 130 pages are packed with 316 favorite recipes from 58 of Lone Star Quilt Shop's quilters. Twenty of their finest quilts are featured in color throughout the book. And the book is wrapped in a concealed spiral binding to help avoid spiral tangles while it keeps all the conveniences of traditional spiral.

· 5¹/₂" x 8¹/₂" · 136 pp · Concealed Spiral

Amish Quilting Cookbook ... Item #733 ... **$14.99**